BOY
DREAMER

BOY DREAMER

AN ARTIST'S MEMOIR
OF
IDENTITY, AWAKENING,
AND
BEATING THE ODDS

PAUL ECKE

WITH
STACEY AARONSON

morrison | meyer

Published 2018

Morrison Meyer Press

Printed in the United States of America

ISBN: 978-1-7323292-0-1 (pbk)

ISBN: 978-1-7323292-1-8 (hc)

ISBN: 978-1-7323292-2-5 (ebk)

Library of Congress Control Number: 2018948238

Book design by Stacey Aaronson

The events and experiences that follow are all true, based on the author's recollection of them. In some situations, names, identities, and other specifics of individuals have been changed in order to protect their privacy.

For my mother,
who loved me unconditionally

And for Bill,
my rock and eternal love

I chew on my nails, a nervous habit I've never broken, waiting for the receptionist to call my name. It is January 21, 2017, and I am my oncologist's first patient of the day.

I've been battling prostate cancer for ten years, seven of which have been with metastasis to my lymph nodes and bones. I've managed it with varying treatments, both integrative and Western. This is merely a routine three-month check to ensure my PSA scores haven't risen.

If you do the right things for your body, for your immune system, you can live with stage IV cancer. I know this because that's exactly what I've been doing for the past decade. I've kept it under control, oddly tolerable, and in some brief—very brief—moments, forgotten.

My doctor welcomes me into her office and hugs me, tells me that she's just arrived, then sits and scans her computer screen with the results of my recent blood draw. The last several checks have been fine, and there's no reason to believe this one will be different. Yet it is only seconds before I see the minute change in her face, that shift from clinical to compassionate, as she closes her eyes for a moment and turns to me.

She sighs and her shoulders fall. "I know you've worked really hard, Paul," she says, softly shaking her head and placing her hand on my knee. "I'm sorry."

Tears immediately well in my eyes as I knowingly nod, my throat too tight to respond. She gently hands me a tissue and then turns to Bill, my partner of nearly forty years, and goes over the test results and treatment options. I know I should be listening, but her voice becomes muffled and distant, an echoey shadow floating around and through me in the stark white room.

. . . elevated considerably . . . go back on hormone deprivation therapy . . . difficult decision . . .

I think about how this slow-growing bastard is fickle. How I can do everything right and it might still taunt me, mock me. Almost everyone in my family has died from cancer, so I believed for a long time that the odds were against me. But I now know, from what's come from the field of epigenetics, that genes rarely play a role, if at all. It's the other things in life that cause tumors to grow, some controllable, like the food we eat, the products we use, the drugs we willingly take, the alcohol we consume. But there are other causes too. Emotional wounds that can only be buried so deep before they tire of being silenced. Erroneous beliefs we hold in our minds. The trauma that we work so hard to "get past" so that we can live a full life.

But unlike what my sisters believe about our childhood, that it's over and there's no use bringing it up now, my past does not live outside of me like something enveloped by time and transmuted into dust. It is part of me, whether I want it to be or not.

The tumors have bobbed steadily, even patiently, in the ocean that is me, awaiting a certain kind of courage to take my hand. Not the courage of battling the cancer, but the courage to acknowledge those wounds, those inflicted injustices and decisions from my past that have caused it. They're tired of lying in wait, of not being heard.

That's what suppression does to people, to cells. After a while, how long no one knows, grievances speak up in the language of disease to tell you that it's no longer okay to cloak the storm in the guise of a cloudless sky . . .

PART ONE

The Canvas

CHAPTER ONE

December, 1957

I wake with a start and bolt upright. I'm up high, too high. Despite the blanket wrapped around me, I shiver as an unfamiliar chest of drawers and metal trash can stare at me. *You're not welcome here,* they seem to say. Looking around, I realize I'm on the top level of a bunk bed. I've never been in one before and I feel stranded. *Where are my sisters?* Gail is fourteen months older than me and Tina is only a year.

Suddenly, I remember our mother explaining to us tearfully the day before that we were going to be staying with another family for a while. It didn't make sense to me, but I imagined it had something to do with my father.

Just then, a woman entered the room. She was drawn with long, narrow strokes and subtle curved lines, and she announced with a curtness that didn't match her prettiness that it was time to get up, get washed, and get dressed. She told me her name was Marge and gave a brief orientation of the morning routine and duties, which included making the too-high bed.

"Breakfast is on the table," she said, clapping her hands brusquely, "so don't waste any time."

I do my best to complete the list of demands, then hurry into the kitchen to find Gail already seated with a bright smile. She sits dutifully with her hands in her lap as I take my seat beside her, my feet dangling nervously as I glance around the table.

"That'll always be your chair," Marge says, turning briefly from the stove.

I nod faintly, relieved that mine isn't next to the stern, pasty man next to Gail, whose name I learn is Ray.

A few thickly silent moments after my arrival, Ray lowers his news-paper to reveal a pair of beady eyes behind heavy black horn-rimmed glasses. He sits stick-straight, his bald head shiny with the reflection of the sun from the window. Painted with thin, sharp lines and the inner darkness of a dense forest at midnight, he is as welcoming as the icy furniture in the bedroom. He locks his eyes on mine, and a piercing chill shoots through my body. I drop my head and freeze, bile creeping up my throat.

"Look at me," he says, his voice like the edge of a dagger.

I keep my head bowed but peer toward him from under my brow.

"You're to eat everything you're served. And you're only to speak when you're spoken to."

The "everything," I quickly discovered, was cereal and milk, and possibly a glass of juice. Eggs, pancakes, bacon, toast, and other morning delights would be reserved for Marge and Ray—and their aptly named princess of a daughter, Regina.

"And," he adds, "it'll be your job to clear the table, you and your sister."

I look tentatively at Gail, whose eyes tell me to keep quiet.

I am four years old.

And this is my first day in a foster home.

CHAPTER TWO

Regina stares at me, her eyes conveying a mixture of resentment and curiosity. She is Gail's age, with a cute freckled face and strawberry-colored hair pulled into tight pigtails, but I can sense instinctively that we aren't going to be friends.

The scents of toast and bacon bob around me like out-of-reach balloons, as I quietly spoon cereal into my mouth. It's not even the fun kind, like Sugar Smacks or Corn-Fetti, but some type of boring flakes. Regina savors each item on her plate, flaunting the fact that she's served something better than we are, as she chats enthusiastically with her parents. Gail and I, who seem to be invisible, remain quiet observers, watching their conversation like a tennis match. That's when I notice the empty high chair in the corner and wonder where Tina is. I don't dare ask, though. I assume she is sleeping and console myself with that.

Once we clear the table as instructed, we are given a list of chores. Gail must complete hers before heading off to school, and I'm not allowed to go outside to play until everything is completed to Marge's approval. I quickly discover that missing an element of the chore means doing it all over again. She or Ray examines every finished task carefully, with the exacting manner of a drill sergeant. I'm not used to this kind of harsh structure; everything about their behavior toward us is cold and abrupt, and I can't understand why. It is clear that the affection they show their daughter is completely lost on us. Even at four years old, I wonder, *How can someone be so kind to their own child and so mean to another?*

It was true that our family was the picture of instability. Yet my sisters and I had played, argued, and spent our days with relative freedom. Meals were simple, joyous occasions. In this rigid environment that was the Fletchers', I immediately longed for my mother's sweet and loving ways, for the comforts of our modest apartment, for the small bedroom I shared with my sisters, for the relatively unstructured lifestyle we took for granted. I imagined I could handle the arguments between my parents and my father's long absences if only we could go home.

I had no idea how long I would have to wait.

————

That first week consisted of drawn-out days with the same routine: chores upon rising; remaining silent during breakfast, eating our cereal while Marge, Ray, and Regina devoured something hot that teased us with its aroma; clearing the table; then chores after breakfast while we were watched like hawks for shortcomings. But perhaps the worst part was that Tina almost never stopped crying. Gail and I did everything we could to try to comfort her, but she simply couldn't bear being away from our mother.

"What do you think we should do about Tina?" I whispered to Gail, as we scrubbed the bathroom floor in tandem.

"I'm trying," Gail snapped, defensive in her self-imposed maternal role. "There's only so much I can do."

I hung my head and continued moving the sponge back and forth, shaken to the core by Tina's crying. Suddenly I heard Marge yell, "Shut up!"

Gail and I rushed into the living room to find Marge shaking Tina violently and yelling at her. We stood frozen as Ray glared at us from the couch, gluing us to the floor with his eyes.

Then Marge smacked Tina as punishment for crying, which only made her cry more. Tears welled in my eyes as I felt my heart crack in two. Our parents never hit us, and I knew deep down that it was wrong, especially since Tina was only a baby. Ray appeared in a flash.

"There'll be no crying in this house, not from either of you," he said, narrowing his eyes at me, then at Gail, who I realized was crying too. "You got that? *No* crying. Ever." His voice was laced with warning and a large crease cracked his forehead in half. "Now go to your rooms and stay there until you're told to come out."

Gail and I turned and dashed away, afraid to even look at each other.

I scrambled to the top bunk and buried my face in my pillow, where I imagined my silent tears magically transforming into a beautiful garden of protection, then blossoming into our escape.

It was hours before anyone came to get us.

CHAPTER THREE

In that first week alone, it was impossible not to know that we were nothing but a nuisance to the Fletchers—if not a nuisance who performed constant labor around the house. We also discovered that breakfast wasn't the only meal at which we were given the inferior version. If Regina was served toasted ham and cheese with lettuce and mayo for lunch, we received a slice of bologna on dull white bread with ketchup; if the family had steak for dinner, we might have a thin hamburger patty with nothing on it. If we didn't like what we were served, there were no alternatives. And if we didn't finish it, Ray or Marge gave us the uneaten portion for the next meal. Like a scene from *Mommie Dearest*, we could face a rare-cooked burger from dinner, the kind with red juice oozing from it, the next morning at breakfast.

What we didn't understand then but came to learn later is that the Fletchers regularly took in foster children strictly for the money. Neither of them worked, and they spent as little on us as they possibly could, reserving their stipend for themselves and their daughter. And because they were always home, Ray's militant gaze and Marge's disapproving manner seemed to follow us wherever we went. What's more, the apple didn't fall far from the tree.

Regina had a treasured playhouse in the backyard, and she sometimes let us play in it with her, but only if we obeyed strict rules. She didn't like us touching or moving anything, and she dictated all the make-believe. This created a certain tension between her and Gail, who by nature liked to be in charge. If Gail displeased Regina, Regina would go outside for a few minutes, then run toward the house.

"Mom!" she'd yell. "Paul pooped behind my playhouse!"

When Marge came out, she would indeed find poop—one of her darling daughter's weapons of choice. Never imagining her princess was lying, we would be reprimanded and sent to our rooms for an indefinite period of time.

This frequent segregation became our daily routine.

With no books or toys to occupy my time, I would escape into a vibrant fantasy world, where anything was possible. I imagined living in a huge, beautiful house on the beach with my family, where the ocean mist playfully sprinkled the windows and beckoned us outside. My mother's hair was swept up in a French roll with curls on top, her matte-red lips smiling as she brought lemonade to us. Her pink and orange floral poplin dress swish-swished with the breeze, and we all laughed as her high heels sank into the sand. She would then kick them off and chase us giggling, falling into the warm sand with us, smothering us with kisses that left scarlet smudges on our faces. Then we would dash into the water and dive under, opening our eyes to dance with the fish. Our hair would billow gently from our heads like soft flames of innocence, as we picked up starfish and compared sizes underwater. We would then set them down in the midst of the ocean-floor plant life, never dreaming of extinguishing their lives by removing them, then return to the beach where our mother would wrap all three of us in a gigantic towel. Rubbing our heads and wiping the lip rouge off our faces, she would tell us how much she loved us, that we meant the world to her. Then she would twirl us, one by one, with her hands clasped safely on our wrists, around and around. The wind and the sun would dry the remaining beads of water from our legs, and we would kick our sand-covered feet as if swimming in air. She would never tire, of course, only let go to allow us to gather our pails and shovels and scramble closer to the water to build a sandcastle. Gail would know just how close we could be without it being threatened by the tide, and Tina would be careful not to topple our handiwork, content to play next to us. As I started on the foundation, I would look up and see my mother lying on her yellow-and-white-striped chaise longue, her large black sunglasses and wide, floppy straw hat, with a nosegay attached to the front, making her look like a movie star.

———

The following weekend, we are told our parents are coming for a visit. Gail and I can hardly restrain our excitement, but when I pass a furtive sparkle-eyed glance her way, she gives me a look that says to keep it contained in silence.

I dress in my favorite outfit, and as I take special care to comb my hair nicely, I imagine us driving to a park, or maybe to the beach, then going out to lunch where we can order whatever we want from the menu. We'll sit outside with a giant umbrella over our table, and our mother will admit that she can't bear to be away from us another minute. Then we'll tell our parents what's been happening at the Fletchers. Once they find out, they'll be in such shock that they'll decide then and there that we won't be going back.

Once they arrive, however, the visit isn't at all what I expect.

Marge and Ray have set up a single chair in the entryway, just inside the door, where my mother is instructed to sit. I'm so overjoyed to see her that I clamber immediately into her lap. My father stands quietly beside her, as if overseeing the whole exchange as a bystander. But when Gail rushes toward him, he scoops her up with a "Hello, darling," distracting him briefly from my time with my mother. It is short-lived, though, because the most attention must be paid to Tina.

She has been nearly inconsolable since we arrived, and when Marge hands her to my mother, she makes it clear that they didn't sign up for such chaos and frustration.

"But she's fine now," my mother says nervously, holding Tina close and rocking her, which calms Tina immediately.

"But that's not how she usually is," Marge counters.

I can tell she's trying to be polite, but there's an edge to her voice that begs for swift resolution.

Having no alternative, my mother gathers every ounce of optimism and declares that Tina will get better, that she just needs a little more time to adjust. Marge is visibly dissatisfied and folds her arms across her chest. "I hope so," she says, smiling curtly with an unconvincing nod before returning to her place next to Ray.

"I'm so happy to see you," I say to my mother, caressing her cheek.

"I'm happy to see you too," she says, kissing me tenderly.

But behind her words I sense a sadness, the resigned melancholy she exhibits after my parents have been fighting. I don't understand how she can be sad when we're together for the first time in over a week, and I can tell that she's trying not to show it, but I see it nonetheless.

"How've you been, sweetheart?" she asks feebly. "Have you been a good boy?"

I shoot a glance at Gail. The Fletchers expressly told us that we were not to share with our parents any of the discipline they doled out to us. I consider breaking the promise not to, but Marge and Ray are watching us from only a few feet away. I'd have to wait until we left to tell her the truth.

"Yes," I say to her. "I've been good."

She holds my face in her hand as she cradles Tina with her other arm. "That's my sweet boy."

I smile. Just hearing her voice is like being covered with the softest blanket.

"So when are we leaving?" I ask.

My mother looks at my father with pain in her eyes.

"We're not leaving," my father says.

"But what about our visit?" I ask. "Aren't we going somewhere?"

Marge approaches swiftly, like a witch swooping in on a broom. "This *is* your visit, Paul. Right here. Now don't go upsetting your mother with your questions."

I look at my mother and she turns to Tina. I can see that tears are filling her eyes, and I begin to cry.

"But I want to go home," I whine. "Why can't we come home?"

Marge claps her hand on my shoulder. "What did I just say? See how you're upsetting your mother?"

And with that Marge pulls Tina away, who immediately begins to scream, and walks out of the entry. It is then it's decided that our meeting is over. My mother can barely look at me; my father puts Gail down, and the next thing I know they are gone. No park, no beach, no lunch under an umbrella. Just a handful of minutes that feel stomped on and broken into pieces.

After my parents leave, I receive harsh punishment for crying in front of them and upsetting my mother. Gail somehow keeps her emotions in check, but I can't manage it. I lie in my top bunk and cry my eyes out, muffling the sound with my pillow almost to the point of suffocation so that Ray, with his acute radar for weakness, won't hear me.

CHAPTER FOUR

Shortly after the first visit with our parents, it is Christmas Eve. Ray and Regina drive off into the crisp, sunny Southern California afternoon and return sometime later with a grand tree, which Ray puts up in the living room. He mumbles a lot as he strings the lights around it, then Regina, who can barely wait until the lights are successfully arranged and tested, excitedly pulls the ornaments out of boxes and places them on the branches with her mother while Gail and I watch.

Besides our parents' visit, it is the first time we feel any degree of excitement. Santa was coming; surely he'd been informed that we were staying in a different house this year. Though we didn't have a special dinner like we always did at home, and though we were sent to bed even earlier than usual, I didn't mind. I lay in my bunk and closed my eyes, a smile spreading across my face as I imagined running to the tree in the morning to discover the base of it surrounded with the toys Santa left us: a pretty blonde doll in a miniature high chair, the kind whose legs and arms moved; Candy Land, Chutes and Ladders, and Colorforms; crayons and a book full of blank paper to draw in; Lincoln Logs, colored blocks, and Tinker Toys; and Barbie dolls with lots and lots of fashionable clothes, just like we saw advertised on TV.

———

When dawn broke with a glorious sun, my eyes popped open. I didn't climb down from my bed, though. Marge had told us we weren't to come out until we were called. So I lay there dreaming of dressing the dolls, and building a big house with the blocks, and sticking and unsticking the Colorforms onto the wall next to my bed. The removable decals would come alive at night and have parties and picnics under a constant sun. "Come on, Paul," they would say, waving me toward them. "You come too." And just like that, I would join their celebration and share their cakes and cookies and lemonade. We would talk and eat and laugh through the wee hours, and no one would ever tell me I wasn't allowed to play because I was a sissy or a baby or liked the same toys the girls did.

"Gail . . . Paul," Marge called, throwing a few curt knocks on our doors. "You can come out now."

We both scrambled out and ran to the living room to find an array of toys around the tree, just the way I imagined, with Regina already planted in front of it. She was playing with a doll as Ray smiled at his little princess from the couch. When I went to pick up one of the toys, Marge grabbed my shoulder and yanked me back. "Those are for Regina," she said. "There are no toys for you and your sisters."

I looked at Gail with confusion.

"But didn't Santa leave anything for us?" Gail asked.

"No," Marge said with a smirk. "Santa doesn't come for children like you."

My entire body deflated. Gail and I looked at each other, fighting back tears. Ray shot us a glare. Marge disappeared into the kitchen to fix breakfast, while we watched Regina play with all the toys we would have loved but that Santa apparently no longer brought to children like us.

———

Time seemed to pass like waiting for the last drop of honey on the bottom to reach the spout, then turning it over and starting the process all over again. Gail and I had no choice but to hastily adapt to living like robots—we took orders, remained largely silent, and learned to suppress emotion in Marge, Ray, and Regina's presence. But poor Tina was too young to conform to their unreasonable rules, and she simply couldn't cope with being separated from our mother. Her constant outbursts and melancholy continued, which only served to ignite Marge and Ray's anger.

One particular morning, Tina sat in her high chair, sniffing and sobbing the way toddlers often show their discontent. Ray fidgeted and shifted, repeatedly snapping his newspaper and peering over it, his lips forming a hard line that curved down abruptly. Finally, when he could take it no longer, he slammed his paper down on the table and leaned toward Tina, his face only inches from hers. "SHUT. UP." I saw spit fly out of his mouth and a rage overtake him as he grabbed my glass of milk and poured it over Tina's head. Tina screamed as the throbbing, sinister gray of his cruelty pulsed through the room and enveloped me like a parasite. The powerlessness I felt rushed through my being like fire, riddling me with anxiety. It took every ounce of strength I had not to lash out at him. But Ray had made it abundantly clear that I would regret any assertion of my opinion, so I was left to stoically observe the abuse.

This cycle repeated itself, each incident stretching out like ashen taffy that was pulled and pulled but never broke, along a seemingly interminable gravel road with no view of the horizon. The only joyful time in our lives was when our parents came to visit, but even that was bittersweet.

Like the first, each subsequent visit occurred on a weekend, a single chair placed in the entryway where my mother would sit. I didn't understand why we couldn't at least gather in the living room, but my parents were only ever allowed a few steps inside the front door. They never questioned it, though, and they also never questioned Marge and Ray's persistent looming presence a few feet away. The result was that we never shared a moment of private time with either of our parents, so our freedom to be completely ourselves was always constrained.

Gail and I both competed for time with our mother, which was usually shared while she held and comforted Tina. If our father accompanied her, which wasn't always the case, Gail would jump into his arms while I hovered close to my mother. If I couldn't be on her lap, I was standing next to her, hugging her arm or relishing hers around me.

As much as Gail delighted in seeing our father, I harbored a degree of fear of him. Whenever he visited, he enthusiastically scooped up Gail, but he never reached out to hug me, or tousle my hair, or show any sign that he was happy to see me. Though he was gifted with the kind of stylish lines that created handsomeness and charm on the outside that drew people to him, he was a blank canvas emotionally, one on which red paint would appear during arguments, then dissipate afterwards. We shared precious few sentimental moments that I remember, and because he was gone so much, we never truly bonded in the way that fathers and sons do. I also witnessed far too many quarrels between him and my mother, and so I grew to see him more as an instigator of pain and sadness than a loving husband and father. Though he never physically abused her or us, the emotional wounds were vivid, and I blamed him for turning my mother into a blubbering mess each time they fought. In short, he was a mystery to me, and I chose tentative detachment and fierce protection of my mother over trying to unravel his perplexing ways.

After the first several weeks at the Fletchers, my father abruptly stopped accompanying my mother on our visits, merely dropping her off for the allotted time. I wondered where he chose to be instead, but I couldn't ask—I had already been admonished about raising questions that might distress my mother. A couple months into our odd visitation routine, however, something unexpected happened.

Despite what my mother hoped, Tina had never acclimated to living with the Fletchers, and her despondence and consistent crying had created misery for everyone. She would scream at the end of every weekend visit, which tore my mother's heart out—and made us fear for Tina once my mother was gone.

But on this particular visit, when Marge swept in to take Tina away, my mother made a calm announcement.

"Tina will be coming with me," she said, holding Tina close. "I've made other arrangements for her."

Gail and I looked at each other wide-eyed. Marge pulled back and raised her eyebrows. "Other arrangements?"

"Yes. My best friend has agreed to take care of her. She can't take all the children because she has a large family of her own, but she can take Tina."

"I see," Marge said, barely able to conceal her elation. She crossed her arms over her chest and shrugged. "Well, if you're certain."

My mother bit her lip as she glanced back and forth between Gail and me, her eyes weighted with anguish that she couldn't take us too.

Though I felt sincere relief for Tina—our "Aunt Jane," as we called her, was a nice lady—I couldn't help but well with tears. My mother wiped the first to fall and held my face in her hand, struggling to hold in tears of her own. "You be a good boy, okay?" she managed.

My face contorted trying to hold in my emotion, knowing I would catch the wrath of Marge and Ray for showing it, but tears streamed down my face.

Marge drew a loud breath. "I'll get Tina's things then." She made haste toward the hall, blowing past Ray, who remained watching like a predator in the shadows.

"Will you still come visit?" Gail asked, her voice cracking.

"Of course, sweetie," my mother said, shifting Tina in her arm and taking her hand from my face to caress Gail's. "You be my strong girl."

Gail nodded with unshrinking obedience. Barely two more words were spoken between us before Marge swept back into the entryway, two bags filled with Tina's things in her hands. "This is everything," she said. She looked out the window and noted my father's car out front. "I guess you'll be going now."

My mother wiped her face and took a deep breath. She stood and hoisted Tina onto her hip, then took the bags from Marge. "I love you," she said to Gail and me, biting her lip again as tears dropped from her jaw onto the front of her brown and cream tweed jacket. Marge guided her out the door like a guest who had overstayed her welcome before we had the chance to cling to her.

"Thank you," I heard my mother say weakly, then she slowly made her way down the steps toward the curb.

CHAPTER FIVE

With Tina gone, the house was definitely quieter, but the forbidding air remained as pungent as ever. Ray and Marge never ceased to hover and threaten, and Regina regularly told lies about us committing one deplorable action or another to get us into trouble.

One day, when I had once again been relegated to my room for something I didn't do, I hatched a risky but delectable plan. I had watched Tina throw tantrums each time my mother left, and though it had taken some time, my mother obviously couldn't take the torment of leaving her baby in that state week after week. Eventually, perhaps through persistent begging or performing a multitude of favors, she had found a more suitable home for Tina. *If I make the same kind of fuss each time she leaves,* I imagined, *maybe she'll find a better home for me too.*

Perhaps it was selfish on my part, but I was operating on survival instinct, not brotherly compassion. The truth was, though Gail was the only reason I felt any sense of security with the Fletchers, our personalities were as complementary as oil and water. As the eldest, she felt a responsibility toward me, a role she had assumed at home in light of our mother's frailty, and it only grew stronger at the Fletchers. Unlike the softness of our mother, which we loved but also witnessed as weakness in the face of our father, Gail felt the need to take on a controlling role, ensuring I didn't break any rules that would get me into trouble. I didn't need a second stern female in my life, and I resented it deeply. But it was Gail's way of protecting me. I didn't see it that way at the time, however, so it became yet another source of my feeling repressed.

Lying in my top bunk, I stared at the mottled white ceiling, my eyes following the sparkly crevices and knolls like an army of ants seeking food. Suddenly, the ceiling cracked open and parted to reveal a wide, smooth, cerulean sky filled with cotton-ball collages of waves, sandcastles, and whales. I stayed in that space for a time, staring up into the life-like puffs, until I saw my father's car pull up to the curb to drop off my mother. As she got out of the car, I noticed her navy blue dress with a white lattice pattern, the seams of her stockings straight up her calves. Her hair curved in all the right places below her pillbox hat, with a delicate veil that seemed to float above. Marge opened the door and my mother stepped inside. Once seated in her entryway chair, and without Tina to tend to, I sat on her lap by myself, while Gail stood by her side. We chatted in our perfunctory but loving way, exchanging kisses and hugs until I saw, through the gauzy drapes, my father's car return. But instead of stuffing my emotion, I started to sob. "Don't go," I begged. "Please. I can't be without you." My mother began to cry but I couldn't let myself feel bad. If she cried, it meant she cared. And if she cared enough, she would find another home where I wouldn't be so miserable. "Paul, my sweetheart," she said, smoothing my hair, "please don't cry." Marge and Ray, for the first time, retreated into the hall where I was certain they were far enough away not to hear me. "It's terrible here," I told her. "They're mean and awful and they're never nice to us." My mother's eyes grew wide. "Mean to you?" she said. Her face softened and hardened at the same time with concern. "Well, we can't have that. You'll have to come home with me. I'll find a way to take care of you, or someone who will, until I get better." I threw my arms around her neck, my chin resting on her shoulder, the cool silk of her dress soothing against my skin, with a smile so enormous I felt my lips burning.

The door flew open. "You can come out now," Marge said, startling me from my reverie. "And hurry up. I have a few chores for you to do."

The following weekend, I am antsy with anticipation for my mother's visit. As I comb my hair and check my outfit in the mirror, I suddenly realize how much I look like my father. I wonder if I remind my mother too much of him, if maybe I'm like him. But I'm not like him, not at all. I know this in my heart, but maybe my mother doesn't know it. I begin to panic and question my plan. If she doesn't take me with her today, I know I'll be harshly punished by Marge and Ray for having an outburst. No, I decide, it's my only hope of escape. I have to take my chances.

When my mother arrives, she tries hard to conceal her typical sadness by hugging us close to her.

"How's Tina?" I ask.

"She's fine," my mother says with a slight smile.

"How are you, Mommy?" Gail asks.

"Oh . . . I'm okay, baby. Tell me what you've been doing."

And the lies begin as always.

We've been playing with Regina in her playhouse . . . kicking the ball around the yard . . . playing Tag and drinking lemonade on the porch . . . playing board games . . .

When the too-short visit comes to a close with the sound of my father's car idling out front, I grab my mother's arm.

"Please don't go." The tears come quickly and naturally. "I don't want you to go."

Marge sweeps in. "Paul," she says sternly, narrowing her eyes. "What is this? How many times do you have to be told not to upset your mother?"

I look at my mother and see that she's crying.

"I'm . . . not trying . . . to upset her," I say in little puffs. "I just . . . want her . . . to stay longer."

Marge looks at my mother. I look at my mother. The silence is interrupted only by her opening her purse with a click and taking out a tissue. She clicks it again and then dabs her cheeks. "I wish I could," she says to me tenderly. "But I really have to go."

My heart moves so rapidly from my chest to my gut that I feel I might throw up.

Gail lightly smacks my arm. "Don't make her feel bad," she says. "She'll be back next week." Then she turns toward our mother. "Right, Mommy?"

"Yes," she says with a brave nod.

"See?" Gail admonishes.

My throat is too tight to make a sound, so I bite my lip hard as my mother rises to leave. I grab the folds of her billowy skirt one more time and bury my face in it. Then I feel Marge yank me away, and I know what's coming.

CHAPTER SIX

May, 1958

After my foiled attempt to leave with my mother, I decided it was best to curtail my emotional outburst strategy and avoid Ray's steely hand. It took a couple months before she found a home fo Tina, and I reasoned it might just take some time for me too. In the meantime, Gail demanded that I not make any more trouble during our family visits or otherwise, so I lapsed back into my robotic routine, hopeful that my mother would be successful soon.

But with each subsequent visit, my mother has no news about finding us a new temporary family, or bringing us home with her. What's more, she is wearing different clothes, looser clothes, than the stylish suits and dresses she typically wears. When I sit on her lap, I have less room; her stomach is rounded and sticking out in the same way it did before Tina came. I don't quite understand, so of course I say nothing, but I see the way Gail looks at her protruding belly and wonder if she knows something I don't.

In June, school ended for Gail and Regina, and the half days they were usually gone during the week became full days together for the summer. Though neither one favored playing with me, having them there was still better than having to brave Marge and Ray all alone.

Over time, Regina and Gail had become reasonably good friends, and I was definitely the odd one out. So while they made believe in the playhouse or had tea parties with dolls in their pretty dresses, I played in quiet corners with the frogs that inhabited the yard, gently holding them and stroking their backs. Despite the fact that Gail and Regina made fun of me, telling me I would grow warts from playing with them, they became my favorite playmates. I named each one and created my own world with those little ribbiting creatures, one where boys and frogs understood each other perfectly and neither wondered if something was wrong with them.

By the time late August signaled that the end of summer was approaching, we had lived with the Fletchers for eight months, and never had we received a single gesture of affection or what you would call a treat. So when Marge announces she is going to bake a cake for my birthday, Gail and I are both elated. I am turning five and about to enter kindergarten, so it feels like a particularly special birthday. I only wish my mother could be there to celebrate with me.

Gail and I hop up to the kitchen table and watch as Marge lets Regina pour the boxed cake mix into the bowl, then add the two eggs and water. Marge lowers the beaters and slowly revs them until they spin at high speed, then scrapes the sides of the bowl with the spatula as the whirring fills the room. When the batter is sufficiently blended, she tilts the head of the mixer back to reveal two chocolate-covered metal treats. She swings the handle on top to pop them out, then hands one to Regina. Gail and I expect to receive the other to share, but instead Marge licks that one herself. Gail and I exchange irked glances but say nothing, as Regina smirks at us and shrugs her shoulders to the tune of "nah-nah-nah-nah-naaah-nah."

After Marge finishes licking the beater like a giraffe with a popsicle, she pours the batter into two round pans and puts them into the oven. Too excited to leave the kitchen while they bake, Gail and I stay at the table and wait, making quiet, idle conversation that won't incite any wrath, as we lean in to see the cakes rise through the oven door window. When the timer ding-dings, Marge rushes in and eases her hands into quilted mitts, then slides the pans out to cool on wire racks.

The scent dances toward us, then cloaks us in a chocolatey vortex that reminds me of home. I close my eyes and imagine myself on a dragon made of cake, his spongy back making for the softest ride, as we fly over the trees and into the clouds, away from the Fletchers forever.

"The cakes have to cool for a while," Marge says, jolting me back to the kitchen, "so you kids go out and play."

We dash outside and I find my usual quiet corner where my frog friends are waiting for me, while the girls rush to the playhouse. About an hour later, Marge calls us in. We tumble into the kitchen where the frosting is sitting on the counter in its little tubs. My stomach leaps with the idea that perhaps Marge has decided that after she ices the cake is when I'll get to lick the utensil.

We settle into our chairs and watch as Marge sets one layer onto a cake plate, then peels off the lid of one tub and swirls chocolate frosting onto the long, narrow spatula. She carefully spreads blob after blob across the top of the first layer, then transfers the other cake to rest on it. She then scoops more frosting and spreads it on top of the bare layer, then smears more around and around the sides until the whole thing is covered. My eyes grow wide imagining the taste of the frosting as it glides off the shiny spatula and onto my tongue. Only she doesn't give the spatula to me. She hands it to Regina with a sickly smile, and Regina licks it in long, mocking strokes as she stares at us. If looks could kill, Regina would be sprawled cold on the floor from the glare I give her when Marge turns her back.

Once the masterpiece is finished, the three of us go back outside to play, but all I can think about is the cake. So I say I have to go to the bathroom, then quietly sneak in through the back door. The cake is sitting there invitingly on the counter, so I tiptoe over to it and take a sweeping look around. The TV is on in the living room, and I guess that Marge and Ray are both watching it. My mouth salivates as my heart hammers a heavy cadence in my chest. I am just tall enough to reach the lowest part, so I gently run my finger along a short stretch of frosting I think no one will notice and poke it into my mouth before anyone can catch me. The sugar practically bursts in my mouth as I swirl my tongue over it; we haven't had anything so delicious since we arrived. Then I gingerly go back outside, careful not to let the door slam.

———

When dinnertime comes, I rush into the kitchen to find the cake in the center of the table. It doesn't matter what inferior meal we're having tonight; whatever Marge serves will be followed by this grand, tantalizing prize for cleaning our plates. We all take our seats as Marge finishes preparing the meal. I'm wriggling in my chair with anticipation and swinging my feet like I'm hurrying somewhere when Regina blurts out, "Who put their finger in the frosting?"

I immediately freeze and feel heat rush to my face. Ray takes one look at me and knows I am the culprit. I look at Gail but her glare is almost as penetrating as Ray's. A long, silent moment passes as Marge comes to the table and practically slams her fists onto her hips.

"Go to your room," Ray barks. "There'll be no dinner for you tonight."

My heart sinks with the weight of a boulder as all eyes bore holes through me. I slide off my chair and run to the bedroom before I can't hold my sobs. I close the door and scramble up the ladder onto my bunk, tears streaming down my face. As my stomach rumbles, I fold the pillow over my face and find solace in the only thing that comforts me: the memory of my mother singing jazz standards to me in her smooth, buttery-vibrato voice that was once featured on the radio, where it rose up into the heavens through the airwaves to sway gently with the stars.

———

That next morning for breakfast, and for every meal after that for three days straight, I am served a slice of chocolate cake. No regular food, only cake, cake, and more cake. Like all other meals in this house, I must eat every last crumb. The beautiful, delicious cake that was supposed to be a celebration for my fifth birthday became a punishment so unreasonable that I couldn't begin to understand it. If the space under the door was large enough, Marge would have slid the cake slices through it, as if feeding a prisoner who had committed a heinous crime. Forbidden to leave my room for any reason, I not only couldn't speak to anyone, but I had to use the cold metal trash can as a toilet.

At night, a sliver of light shone into my room from the hallway, and I could hear Gail crying as she peered under the door. I was surprised she would take a chance like that, and I didn't dare talk to her. Instead, I resorted to burying my face in my pillow, frightened that I would be severely reprimanded for making a sound. With my eyes swollen shut from crying, I escaped into the only world I knew, the one where giant beanstalks grew magically from cake crumbs, pressing against bedroom doors with their thick branches so that dreadful adults couldn't enter, allowing trapped little boys to climb up and up and up, where cloud ferries awaited to transport them to magnificent houses with eaves, and gables, and covered porches with swings, where mothers always sing joyously, fathers always speak in a kind voice to their wives and children, and nobody minds if you swipe a tiny taste of frosting from the only fifth birthday cake you'll ever have.

CHAPTER SEVEN

September, 1958

My mother's visits had become sporadic, and I decided it must have something to do with her expanding belly. On our last several visits, I couldn't even sit on her lap anymore, and she seemed more melancholy than ever. My father had accompanied her on a few occasions, but mostly we hadn't seen him much over the summer. I was inconsolable when she didn't show up, but to avoid the fury of Marge and Ray over any display of sadness, as well as threats of stopping visitation with our parents altogether, I focused on counting down the days that I would finally be starting school.

I wasn't unfamiliar with the classroom environment; I had attended a Head Start preschool program the prior year for underprivileged kids, but Gail told me that kindergarten was different. I didn't know what she meant, but I was about to find out.

The morning of my first day, I put on my favorite outfit and combed my hair with particular precision. Gail and I ate our usual cereal and milk, and then we walked with Regina to the bus stop. While we waited, Regina flaunted her trendy new lunch pail with a princess design pressed into the sides, then flipped it open to reveal a matching thermos nestled against a hearty sandwich, an apple, a bag of chips, and a package of cookies.

"My mommy let me pick it out special," Regina said, tilting her head back with a smirk.

Gail and I glanced down at the small brown bags with our names printed boldly on the side with a black marker, knowing the food inside would have no resemblance to Regina's, as the bus roared up and chugged to a stop.

Despite Regina's smugness, Gail scrambled up the steps and followed her to a pair of seats toward the back, leaving me to take a seat alone. I chose one by the window, then was startled by a blast of sound. I turned to see a short, pudgy woman with cropped gray hair pressing a giant white megaphone against her face.

"THERE WILL BE NO LOUD TALKING ON THE BUS. KEEP YOUR VOICES DOWN AT ALL TIMES. AND NO ONE IS ALLOWED TO STAND UP OR SWITCH SEATS AT ANY TIME."

I turned around to look at the other kids as she continued laying down rules in her boisterous, gravelly voice, making it clear that she would dole out harsh discipline to anyone who disobeyed.

Swiveling back, I stared out the window until we made another stop. A few more kids filed onto the bus and one girl sat next to me. I offered her a slight smile, then faced the window again.

During the ten-mile drive, the brakes screeched and the yellow behemoth lurched forward to a stop multiple times to pick up children along the way. Each time, the driver stood and made her grating pronouncements about the rules and the penalties for breaking them, before grinding the gears and revving onto the road once again. The repetition of this routine, along with the constant chatter of the other kids in varying pitches and fragments that wafted toward me in ripples, wore on my nerves, so I focused my attention out the window.

I had a glorious ocean view, and the sun shone on my face, warming my small frame. I watched the giant waves of the Pacific crash on the sand, fascinated by the spray of the swells and the way the water washed in and out, creating a soft, white foam like a blanket on the shore. The rhythm and motion of the sea put me in a trance-like state, as if my mother was holding me snugly, rocking me in her arms on a sunny day.

When we finally reached the school parking lot, the driver instructed us to take turns filing out row by row into the aisle, then ushered us out the door. Once outside, school attendants directed us to numbered areas on the playground where we would line up each day. As I scurried toward mine, I felt I looked nice and blended in well with the other children my age. Then, glancing around, I noticed that all the other kids had fancy lunch boxes like Regina's. I looked down at my brown bag, clutched in my hand like a glaring symbol of inferiority, and wished I could hide.

"Your teachers will take you to your classrooms now," someone announced. I popped up on my toes and saw a group of female teachers lined up in front of us, several of whom were young and pretty. My eyes lit up as I scanned them and wondered which one would be mine. Just then, a gray-haired woman painted with wide, dark strokes and facial grooves stepped forward and claimed our group.

"My name is Mrs. Secker," she practically growled, "and I expect you all to be obedient. I won't put up with anything less." She glared sternly down the line as if to drive her point home, then led us to our classroom where we were instructed to sit on the carpet, Indian-style.

"There will be no fidgeting, and absolutely no talking unless you're called upon," she barked. "You're always to raise your hand, and you may only speak when I call on you."

I took a surreptitious peek over my shoulder and saw that the other kids looked as petrified as I did. In my Head Start program, we were encouraged to interact with each other, as long as we used quiet voices. Here, however, we might as well have been attending school in the Fletchers' living room, with all the coldness and intimidation offered up to us on plates of rigid rules.

In preschool, because I had a short attention span and was naturally talkative, it took me a while to get used to speaking softly and not in my usual playground voice. I had also found it difficult to focus in any learning center that had to do with reading and comprehension, as well as with numbers and mathematical equations. I was constantly frustrated and easily distracted, but all of that changed when I was exposed to the art center.

Drawing and painting came so naturally and with such delight that I felt something shift inside me. To be able to use paints, crayons, and colored chalk, along with scissors, paper, and paste was something I savored as much as pressing milk chocolate into the roof of my mouth, then swirling it around with my tongue to relish its sweetness. The more I explored using the different materials, the more adventurous I became.

After preschool ended, I craved the joy of being immersed in art projects, but Ray and Marge had barely allowed us to use coloring books. Because the crayons left waxy remnants, we had to constantly make sure none got on the table or fell onto the floor, which took most of the fun out of it. But Gail had often brought drawings and construction-paper crafts home from kindergarten, so I had every reason to hope I would get to do the same.

The first several days of school, despite her brusqueness, I rushed to sit in the front row at Mrs. Secker's feet. When I knew an answer to a question, I would enthusiastically raise my hand. If she called on me, I would speak in my overexcited voice. This got me sent to the corner multiple times, which was actually one of the less humiliating punishments in Mrs. Secker's repertoire. Never one to conform or follow strict rules very well, I was getting ample practice both at home and at school. But in the classroom, with the energy of the other kids around me, I simply couldn't temper my voice and enthusiasm all the time, so the corner became a familiar view on any given school day.

While the classroom felt repressive in many ways, and art projects weren't as plentiful as I imagined, the playground was my escape into wide open space. Here I could run, hop, and skip with little fear of being disciplined. I loved the relative freedom recess afforded me, where I could choose to partake in various activities or none at all. But one in particular grabbed my attention.

With its sturdy triangular silver frame and chains that squeaked with their own brand of laughter, the swing set stood like a grand, exhilarating transport to the sky. There seemed to be no limit to how high a person could go, and with only ten or so seats, I quickly discovered it was a race to see who could make the first group.

Once on the swing, the recess monitor gave us each a starting shove, and then it was up to us to pump as high as we could for the one hundred seconds that made up a turn. Because I was small, I was also light, and I soared lightning fast without much effort.

"One! Two!" the kids in line started counting, but their voices rapidly faded as I flew out and over them, the weightless euphoria consuming me, my little legs taking me so high that the playground shrank with its inhabitants into a miniature town of tiny-voiced villagers over which I was king. I wore a plush purple robe that lightly dusted the ground, its inside and collar the softest cream velvet. Underneath my robe was the finest clothing, with carved buttons on my shirt, vest, and pants, like royalty in fairy tales. My black wingtips, the fancy kind adults wore, were polished to the highest shine, and their sparkle complemented the jewels in my crown. I would stand on the balcony of my oceanside castle and gaze upon the villagers gathered below, repeating the words to them my mother would say to me. "You are all loved and very special," I said. "You can be whatever you set your mind to. Always believe that. There are no limits to what you can accomplish." Then I continued. "You will always have freedom in my beach kingdom. You can build sandcastles all day if you want to, and I'll give prizes for the best ones. And you can draw and paint as much as you like, and I'll put your pictures up on the castle wall for everyone to come and see. You will all become as rich as I am, and you'll live in beautiful houses by the sea. I'll bake each of you a cake for your birthday, and you can lick all the extra batter and frosting. And we'll have the tallest Christmas tree right here on the beach, and there will be presents for everyone underneath. We'll have a long, long table set up along the shore, where everyone has a seat, and I'll serve you the most delicious Christmas meal, with turkey and stuffing and potatoes and gravy . . . and bread with melting butter. And we'll have all kinds of pies . . . pumpkin and apple and berry and pecan, with whipped cream and ice cream. And everyone will talk about their day, and we'll all listen to each other. And then my helpers will deliver your gifts to you, and we'll take turns opening them. And when all the gifts are opened, we'll play together until midnight, and then we'll go back to our houses to wait for Santa to come. And then we'll all have our own special Christmas morning with our families, with pancakes and bacon and eggs—"

98! 99! 100!

The whistle blew. "Okay, Paul," the monitor called out, "it's time to stop now."

If we went over by three seconds, we would be banned from the swing set for a week. So I pumped one last time to thrust myself higher, then reluctantly dragged my shoes through the sand on my way down, slowing back and forth to a hazy stop. As I looked out at the faces staring at me, I begrudgingly left my magic transport, wishing that one hundred took much longer to count to, and that my robe and castle and riches didn't only reside in the sky.

———

A few weeks after school started, my mother resumed her weekend visits. Though she was still wearing baggy clothes, I noticed right away that there was more room on her lap than there had been the last time. I didn't ask why, and she didn't offer an explanation; we simply picked up where we left off, with her valiant effort to hide her despair and my enthusiasm to bury myself in her softness.

What I didn't know is that my mother had spent the past nine months in a mental hospital. After numerous ongoing fights between her and my father, caused by his frequent womanizing, extended absences, and squandering of our finances, she had slowly slipped into a deep depression. But her addiction to my father's charm was irrepressible, and in a night of renewed passion, they had conceived another child. This sent her into a downward spiral that was her breaking point, and with her last shred of stability, she checked herself into a sanitarium. It was at this point that our father—presumably out of desperation and with little knowledge of the character of the family—had found the Fletchers to take us in, and because my mother was a voluntary patient, she was able to leave as she pleased to attend our weekend visits. Fragile and carrying the weight of a nervous breakdown—and a fourth child—she had done her best to retain consistent contact with us and maintain some semblance of sanity. It had broken her heart to be separated from us, but she felt she had no choice but to try to heal—and give birth—in a controlled environment.

But the arrival of the baby—another girl—was the beginning of yet another tormenting phase for my mother. Because she was still unwell, she arranged for her new daughter to stay with our Aunt Jane, where Tina was, to bide some time. But after three months, she was still unable to bring us home or care for any of us, and my father—though reluctantly—thought it best to give up the baby for adoption. He found a home for her, but because he and my mother both held out hope of having all of their children back, they refused to sign the papers to make the adoption official. It wasn't until a year later that they finally gave up their parental rights to a daughter they dearly loved but would never know.

———

Three more months passed, and life continued as repressive as ever with the Fletchers. Our mother remained a voluntary resident at the mental hospital, and we continued to see her only on weekends. My father sporadically joined her, which carried its own hope and excitement, but I still maintained an irrational fear of him.

School was challenging, not only because I was ceaselessly chatty, but because I persistently struggled with the basics. I did make some friends in my class, but the only time I truly enjoyed school was during art projects or on the playground.

The swings became my genie in a bottle. When the bell rang, I would dash out, obeying the rules to ensure my place in line. If I didn't make the first group, I would count as high as I could while I waited. Though numbers were never my strong suit, I learned over time to count with the other kids to one hundred. Then, as soon as it was my turn, I would pump myself to the highest point, unleashing my wishes in a flurry of imagination. Soaring above the schoolyard, with nothing to hold me back, I would often float into the comfort of a modest, but lovely house in which I had my own room, with enough art supplies to create whatever I wished, with the ocean whispering outside my window, and my family gathered around the table for meals, chatting and laughing and shoving each other for the last roll, or arguing over who did something best, and collecting shells and water-worn rocks during explorations in the sand, and playfully running up shore when the tide came to greet me, then chasing it as it swished and rolled away. And the feeling of safety that comes when your father puts a gentle arm around your mother's waist as she mixes something on the stove, or drapes his arm over her shoulder as they settle on the couch to watch *The Ed Sullivan Show* or *Father Knows Best*, or twirls her around in the living room as a record spins on the turntable, one whose rhythm and lyrics place them in a pocket of time and space where only they seem to exist.

Day after day, defying gravity, I uncorked the genie to fulfill these simplest of wishes as I climbed ever higher toward the clouds, where all things were possible for five-year-old boys, for one hundred seconds of bliss.

———

School let out and Christmas neared, and Gail and I had no reason to believe this year would be any different from the last. We had resigned ourselves to watching Regina open all the presents Santa brought her while we received none, but on Christmas morning, Regina greeted me with a surprise.

"I have something for you," she said, pushing a small box toward me. It was wrapped in pretty paper like the rest of the gifts, and I felt my heart skip. Though I didn't quite trust the look on her face, I was accustomed to Regina looking smug the majority of the time, so I shrugged it off and sat down on the floor.

I carefully unwrapped the box, then lifted the lid. Inside lay a dead frog, one of my treasured friends from the yard. My eyes welled with tears as Regina and Gail burst out laughing. I looked up to see Ray sneering from his corner of the couch while Marge smirked in her chair, the one that matched her with its ugly print and threadbare corners.

I quickly replaced the lid and dashed out of the living room. Safely behind my closed door where I doubted anyone would follow me, I gently lifted the frog out of his box and held him tenderly against my face, tears dripping onto his sweet, textured back, as my tortured heart eked out a good-bye so painful that I was certain it would never fade.

And I was right.

CHAPTER EIGHT

March, 1959

It was a crisp, sun-filled Saturday stretched under a pale blue sky. The leaves giggled above me as I leaned against the trunk of a steadfast white alder, its bark like the sandpapery arm of a friend. Two pairs of bulging eyes stared up at me from their olive green bodies, their necks billowing in and out like sails.

"Gail! Paul!" Marge called out into the backyard.

I exhaled loudly with a slump of my shoulders and gave each confidant a gentle stroke with my finger. Gail hurried past as I pulled myself away from the temporary freedom I was reveling in, worried what we would be blamed for this time, and went inside.

Marge was standing in the kitchen with an odd look on her face. "You need to tidy up and pack your things. You're going home."

Gail and I looked at each other with incredulity.

"We are?" Gail said.

"Yes," Marge confirmed, her mouth tightening to mask her inner happiness with her usual sternness. "Your parents are on their way."

For the last fifteen months, we had felt like prisoners with scant hope for parole, left to wonder what we could have done to deserve such a harsh sentence at our tender ages, if we were the reason our mother was sick, if we would ever be a real family again. No one had ever mentioned when we would go home, if we ever would—not the Fletchers, and not our parents. So this sudden pronouncement that our mom and dad were coming to get us seemed almost too good to be true.

"Well?" Marge said, her hands plopped onto her hips, "what are you waiting for? Go on." She flicked her arm toward us in a shooing motion, and, suddenly certain she wasn't merely tricking us to get our hopes up, we dashed like shot-off firecrackers into our rooms.

Normally particular about folding my clothes just so, I couldn't shove my clothes into my bag fast enough. Then I crashed into Gail racing to the bathroom, where we jockeyed for the sink. I lathered my hands and face as if toiling to start a fire with a stick, then rinsed and dried with the same briskness. I leaned left then right then left again, trying to comb my hair with Gail bobbing around in front of me. Then I rushed back into my room to grab my bag and wait in the entry.

As I stood there, my heart leaping with anticipation, a montage like a movie reel rushed through my mind, flashing frame by frame, of all the times I had envisioned this day. Weeping in my bunk. Soaring on the swings. Riding the bus with my face pressed to the window, wishing the waves could wash me away from the Fletchers and into my mother's arms once again.

Within minutes Gail was there, with her bag and the same wide smile I had plastered on my face.

"So you're leaving, huh?"

Gail and I spun around to find Regina standing there.

The TV chattered at Ray in the living room, and the low, thump-y sounds of Marge opening and closing cabinets in the kitchen echoed through the wall.

"Uh huh," Gail said.

Regina registered a slight look of disappointment, holding on to it briefly, as if having a sister hadn't been so bad after all, then seemed jolted by the memory of whose daughter she was. "Okay, then. See ya," she said, turning on her heel with a shrug and a wave.

Minutes later, we heard a car pull up.

Gail and I began bouncing as if on stationary pogo sticks as footsteps clapped on the walkway, then nearly burst when the knock came.

I opened the door to find my father in a custom-fit suit and tie, his slicked-back hair shiny as patent leather. He had a five o'clock shadow that added to his bad-boy charm, making him look handsomer than ever.

"Daddy, Daddy!" Gail bounded into his arms, smothering him with kisses. "You're here!"

I peered around my father, wondering where my mother was. Squeezing past the jamb, I stepped out onto the porch. A '55 Lincoln Continental sat in the driveway like a proud persimmon-colored splurge from winning big on *The $64,000 Question* or *Twenty-One*. Just then, the window eased down and my mother reached out a hand and waved, her bright red fingernails glistening in the sunlight. Her hazel eyes were hidden behind large black sunglasses, and her hair was swept up in a fashionable bun, with a color-splashed scarf tied loosely under her chin.

"Come on," she called with a twirl of her hand, her apple-red lips that matched her nails trimming her broad smile.

I clutched my bag and ran to her as she threw open the door. She scooped me into her arms and I wrapped mine around her neck, tears of joy pouring down our cheeks.

"Are we really coming home?" I asked, pulling away to look at her.

She wiped my face and nodded. "Yes, my sweet boy. We're going home."

My father slid into the driver's seat as Gail and I scampered into the back. I grasped the front seat and pulled myself forward, placing my hand on my mother's shoulder. She patted it and smiled at me as the showboat rolled down the driveway. It curved into the street, then my father shifted the arm on the steering wheel, lurching us slightly backward, then smoothly and gallantly forward, as I turned to see the Fletchers' house disappear into the afternoon haze.

Neither Marge nor Ray ever bothered to say good-bye.

My mother lit a cigarette, leaving a heavy red smear on the tip, and exhaled the first deep puff out the window as we sailed down Pacific Coast Highway. Relishing the breeze caressing my face, I watched my mother repeatedly tilt her head back and inhale, then blow the smoke out in a galloping streak, as if releasing every remnant of unhappiness, every torment of imprisonment, we had shared in our own way for months.

Bobby Darin sang something about shark bait as we arched over a canal into a small seaside village, ending at a quaint red beach cottage that faced the water. The backseat springs squeaked and propelled us upward as my father bounced into the driveway and screeched to a stop.

"Is this our house?" I blurted.

"Yep," my father said, pulling the keys from the ignition and giving them a jingle.

Gail and I yanked on the handles and shoved open the heavy doors of the convertible, skidding on the grass as we scrambled to the front door.

My mother emerged from the passenger door like Elizabeth Taylor, in her tangerine suit with large pearlescent buttons and a checkered trim down the front and around the collar. Her black high heels gave an extra three inches to her 5'4" frame, and her dark glasses sat regally upon her Roman nose. My father strutted around with a prideful grin and slid his arm into the crook of my mother's, escorting her up to the porch.

When he opened the door, it was like entering a time warp—as if all the tears, and fears, and longing of the past fifteen months had morphed into this glorious structure, a shining result of my ceaseless visions of what could be. Gail and I darted from room to room, squealing "Oh my gosh!" and "I can't believe it!" When we returned to the living room, our parents were sitting snugly on the couch, my father's arm draped across my mother's shoulders, her legs crossed at the ankles. A balloon of joy expanded within me as my new reality settled in. Then my mother gestured with her head to a point beyond me, and I turned to see a set of sliding glass doors. I ran over to discover that they led out to a deck, our very own suspended cradle above the sea. I stepped out and steadied myself against the railing, then hung my head over the waterway. Taupe-colored barnacles and ash-toned mussels hugged the canal walls, while large coral crabs peeked partially out from low tide. I took a deep breath and let the saltwater air replace every breath I had taken at the Fletchers, imagining how much freedom I now had to explore.

The next day, we brought Tina home, and it seemed nothing could tear our family apart ever again.

CHAPTER NINE

The next three years in our Sunset Beach house were like the dawn of a new era. While the myriad wounds of our time at the Fletchers defined my identity in their own distorted way, and the fear of going back into foster care at any time was never far from my mind, living on the water offered an unparalleled rebirth for my five-year-old spirit.

My parents continued to have their ups and downs, and my mother still projected signs of fragility and emotional weakness, but it was by far the happiest we had ever been. Though my father worked long hours and was rarely present to share the responsibilities of bringing up a family, my mother was deeply committed to raising us with plentiful affection and freedom, and there was no doubt that each of us were her treasures.

When my father was home, it seemed to buoy up my mother in the face of her sometimes lingering depression—so much so that it wasn't long before the telltale rounding of her belly began anew. This time, though, with my mother's improved mental state, the pregnancy was cause for celebration, one that all of us reveled in. The fact that the baby was due around Christmas made it all the more exciting.

I desperately wanted a brother, picturing all the fun we might have together, but I also couldn't help but think of the sister my parents gave away. We occasionally talked about her, wondering what she might be doing or what her family was like, but mostly it was an unspoken emotional burden I imagine resided in both my parents like a plague that had no cure.

With our freedom restored, we would awaken at the crack of dawn and eagerly await our mother's permission to explore the coastal backdrop that was now our playground. I spent countless hours running carefree along the shore, my arms outstretched, imagining the wind lifting me, higher, higher. When the tide was low, I would wade into the canal, fascinated by the crabs with their jerky meandering and front-heavy pincers that seemed to defy balance. Squatting down to observe them, I would softly sweep the water with my hand as I patiently watched and waited, then stand when the tide moved higher and gently trudge through the sea-floor silt. A boulder rested near the canal wall, and it was the perfect spot to sit and contemplate catching one of the exotic creatures.

The first time I tried, I reached out numerous times as one shimmied up the canal wall, attempting to touch its carapace, but the claw would always snap and I would snatch my hand away. When I finally succeeded in picking it up, its flailing legs reminding me of a tantrum, I encoded my technique so that I could repeat the challenge on a daily basis without being pinched.

When I wasn't playing junior crab hunter or delighting in the ocean spray that tickled my face and limbs, peppering my skin with sand magnets, I was building grand airplanes among the dirt tepees scattered throughout the swampland behind our house. Construction workers were attempting to erect something there that seemed to require numerous patches of inaction, and I would take the orange-tipped sticks they used to site the property to construct make-believe airplanes, then hide behind the tall mounds to embark on my sky-borne explorations. All things were possible when tucked between those looming rockets of dirt, where planes made of simple pine sticks could fly.

———

One morning, my father announced that we were going clamming together. I didn't know exactly what that meant, but the idea that my father wanted to do something with me was like a helium infusion straight to the heart. He rolled up his pants and kicked off his shoes, then led me by the hand with a pail in the other out to the canal.

"Now this can be tricky," he said. "See how they disappear into the sand when the tide rolls back?"

I nodded.

"Now see the little hole they leave?"

I bent down and put my finger into one.

"Yep. That's one."

I stood up, beaming.

"Once they hide like that, we have to dig down to get them out. I'll show you."

I gave rapt attention to my father's technique, how he waited for the tide to recede, then scooped the sand quickly with one hand, while his thumb and fingers of the other constricted like a crescent wrench around the shell, then hauled it up and set it in the pail. After a few successful nabs, it was my turn.

His bare feet moved carefully in the swirling foam. I mirrored him as he scanned the area before the water hurried away. "There," he pointed. "I'll dig and you pull it out."

I squatted as my father dug with both hands this time.

"Now!" he said. "Get it!"

I reached down, but the clam burrowed a little deeper. I looked up at my father.

"It's okay," my father said with a lighthearted chuckle. "They do that sometimes." I gave a slight smile as he patted my shoulder. "I'll help you."

At that moment, I wasn't a child separate from the man I couldn't relate to. We were a team, connected, sharing a task of togetherness that spelled bond, as he placed his hand over mine and we captured the clam as a single entity.

Besides the times I had innocently bathed with him as a toddler, leaning against his chest and petting the wet hair on his arm with my fingertip, where he taught me how to squirt water through my hands while I giggled, this was the closest I ever felt to him.

It became the one thing we did as father and son that didn't have a barrier between us, one that was invisible to the eye but keenly felt, as if we stood on opposite sides of a rushing highway whose gale warned that neither one of us could cross without vulnerability and awkwardness, a risk neither of us was willing take.

————

When school ended that June, I received shattering news: I would not be moving on to first grade. With subpar reading and math skills, and a level of immaturity that matched, it was decided that I should repeat kindergarten. Reduced to full-body sobs, I begged my mother not to hold me back. I could envision all the children that next year pointing and laughing at me, the one kid who was left behind. I had been left behind before, and my heart couldn't take another dose of it.

But no amount of crying or begging changed my parents' minds.

"Don't feel so bad about it, sweetheart," my mother said, scooping me onto her lap and smoothing my hair. "This will give you a chance to catch up. And then first grade will be so much easier for you."

She may have been right, but all I could see was the ridicule, the intense embarrassment of being older than all the other kids in my class, of it being that way for the rest of my life. It was worse, even, than being sent to the liquor store with a note so that I could buy cigarettes and feminine products for my mother when she didn't have the strength to do it herself.

The only consolation to the summer ticking down until I entered kindergarten for the second time was learning to swim in the canal. I took to each type of stroke and kick immediately; propelling myself through the water like a tiny torpedo was the most free I'd ever felt. Not even cracking my head open on a concrete pillar, sending me to the hospital for dozens of stitches, deterred me. I would hold my breath as long as I could underwater, making a game of it, imagining myself growing gills so that I could explore the depths of a mystical world unknown to me.

After I mastered the safe haven of the canal, I moved into the challenge of the ocean. Feeling lured by something deep inside me, the ocean was an intriguing mystery, seducing me to ride the waves I had dreamed and dreamed of as I soared on the playground swings. I would close my eyes and travel in my mind to a distant land, bobbing and swaying with each undulation like a small but fortified ship, open to whatever destination my magical inner captain would take me to. In the water, I wasn't abandoned, or rejected, or sad, or trapped the way I had been at the Fletchers—that in certain ways I would be my entire life. The ocean allowed me to feel wholly supported, protected yet free, comforted and encouraged to be me. Just me.

When the beach's call would awaken me from my explorations, the shimmering grains waving me in like scores of tiny playfellows to carve them into pieces of art, I would swim to the shore and tumble onto the sand. Hours elapsed like minutes as I formed and patted and sculpted pails upon pails of minuscule pebbles into an estate of sandcastles, always disappointed when the sun would slowly begin to set on their towers and turrets, signaling that it was time to pack up and go inside.

Tomorrow would beckon me to the same divine routine, eager to discover what new adventure awaited me on the shore and in the sea, until the last of the summer days saw its final sun drop beyond the horizon.

———

Though I never truly adjusted to a repeat round of kindergarten, I did learn to better grasp the basics that had eluded me my first year. Looking back, it's no wonder I couldn't concentrate. I never knew if my imprisonment with the Fletchers and scrutinized weekend visits with my parents would stretch out ahead of me until I graduated from high school. But here, in our beach house, with possibly a brother on the way, and my parents getting along the majority of the time, a spark of hope elevated me. Nothing would ever quench my loquaciousness, or my deep need to create art over all other subjects, or the worry that if we made my mother sick again, we might have to be sent away. But if my father believed I could be his partner in something as seemingly simple yet precisely timed and executed as unearthing clams from their sandy hideouts, perhaps I indeed had the ability to accomplish anything, just like my mother always told me.

That Christmas Eve, my mother went into labor, and the next day, we found out that we had another sister, a baby my parents fittingly named Noel Christine.

CHAPTER TEN

Though my age didn't match my schoolmates', my smallness helped me to not stand out as much as I might have otherwise. What did isolate me, however, was the fact that I had virtually no ability to play the way the other boys did. It wasn't just that neither Ray nor my father had ever taught me to throw, catch, or kick a ball, making me feel naturally inferior, it was that I had zero desire to play sports of any kind. I not only hated the act of participating, but I also despised the spirit of competition. To avoid the teasing and sneers of the other boys, I showed off in the areas where I excelled, like the monkey bars or rings. The boys called me names for doing the activities that mostly drew the girls, but having the girls on my side was much better than being a complete outcast.

Sometime in second grade, our family got a puppy. But fairly quickly, what was meant to be the family dog became *my* dog. She accompanied me on my swampland flights, my shoreline fancies, my nighttime trips into dreamland, nuzzled beside me as I slept. It was perhaps the first time I felt a kinship with anyone as deeply as I did with my mother. My sisters didn't seem to mind that I assumed all the responsibility for her, and I took great pride in providing for her every need.

Misty was the recipient of all I had longed for in foster care: compassion, understanding, a playmate. I always spoke to her in a loving, nurturing voice, and I heaped as much affection on her as she would tolerate. When she looked into my eyes, she wasn't a dog at all; she was a soul mate who saw how easy it was for me to feel threatened, to feel that early-imprint fear that was nearly consuming. When I got in trouble, I would run outside and hide behind one of the giant dirt cones, Misty by my side. She seemed to hate seeing me upset, and I treasured how she empathized so completely with only her spirit to convey it.

One day, I was walking her down our street when she suddenly darted away from me, the leash ripping from my hand. I guessed she had seen another animal; she'd never dashed away with such force before. But by the time I turned to call for her, I heard the screech of brakes and a thump accompanied by a piercing cry. A man jumped out of the car as I ran into the street. I fell to the ground and put my hand on Misty's fur, but she wasn't moving. As I carefully picked her up, I could innately sense that there was no life in her. Not understanding death, I thought that medicine or a trip to the hospital could make her breathe again, but the look on the man's face didn't support my naïveté.

"I'm so sorry, son," he said. "It happened so fast. I tried to stop." His voice cracked a little, and I studied his face. I could tell he felt bad, but I could also tell that he had no idea what he had just taken from me.

That night, after we buried Misty in a box in the yard near one of my airplanes, I curled up in my bed and sobbed as intensely as I had when my fifth birthday was ruined, when my mother didn't rescue me from the Fletchers when I felt certain she would, when one of my beloved frog friends was delivered to me, shriveled and devoid of life, in a box. Somehow, however, this despair wracked me at an even deeper level, one that felt like I had just buried a piece of my own soul.

———

By the time I was in the fourth grade, the beach house was a distant memory. We had moved twice by then, and my parents had separated, seemingly for good. Having moved in with his mistress across town, my father rented us a compact apartment in a massive complex called Broadway Village. Somewhere in the neighborhood of five hundred families lived there, mostly single mothers with a passel of undernourished children, and everything from the paint to the faucets dripped low-income.

Except for Gail's room.

Not long before, Gail had come down with an illness. My mother thought it was just the flu that was going around, but it wasn't until the pain in Gail's abdomen became unbearable that my mother realized it was something more. After rushing her to the hospital, she was told Gail had acute appendicitis and that she was very close to dying.

We kids weren't allowed at the hospital, so we huddled under the swirl of gray that hovered over our apartment, awaiting word of her surgery. When the phone call came that she made it through, a buoyant shade of pink filled us all with relief.

Though both my parents were distraught over Gail's sickness, my father was particularly torn apart. She was his little princess, and the idea of losing her nearly put him over the edge. So in celebration of Gail's recovery, my father bought her a lavish bedroom set, complete with a canopy bed, vanity with mirror, and large dresser all for her. That fact that we only had two bedrooms in our apartment didn't faze him in the slightest.

So, for reasons that still confound me, Gail reigned in her solitary castle while Tina, Noel, and I, along with our mother, shared the other bedroom, all of us sleeping in the same bed. The imbalance of this arrangement was like a boulder on one side of a teeter-totter with a feather on the other. But Gail was daddy's little girl, and though he wouldn't deign to live in a tenement himself, he at least made sure his eldest wasn't the peasant at the ball.

Gail's room was off limits to me, of course. She was fastidious about having her things just so, and she didn't want her brother messing with them. But Gail's Barbies were too powerful a magnet for me. Anytime she was gone, or even outside playing with friends, I would sneak into her room and spirit away her Barbies and Kens and their irresistible fashion collection to a secluded spot between her bed and the wall. There, I would dress and undress them, whispering advice on which pieces looked best together, then hold glamorous runway shows. When they weren't modeling the latest ensembles, I pretended they were a family, chitter-chattering with slight twisting gestures, making decisions on my behalf.

"I think Paul should have his own room, don't you?"

"Of course I do. Every boy should have his own room."

"It's too bad he has to hide to play with his sister's dolls. She always gets so mad when she catches him."

"That's why he should have his own room with his own Barbies."

"I agree. And he knows so much more about fashion than Gail does."

"I bet he'll be a famous fashion designer one day."

"I bet he will be too."

Every time Gail caught me, she would yank me by the arm and launch into her usual tirade, complete with shouting, flailing arms, and her admonishment to stay OUT of her room and to stay AWAY from her Barbies, followed by "MOM! Paul is in my room A-GAIN!"

I think deep down, my mother found it amusing that I risked my limbs and hearing to fraternize with Gail's Barbie dolls, but she'd attempt to punish me in her weary way just the same. I was usually dashing out the door by then, dodging her sweeping arm in a lackluster effort to swat me, speeding down the stairs into the courtyard.

———

Though my parents weren't officially divorced, my father rarely came to visit, and when he did, he was often drunk. That, coupled with my mother's movie-star glamour long ago replaced by excess weight, a handful of multicolored muumuus, and a broken front tooth that made her resort to covering her mouth when she smiled, meant that there were no longer volatile but romantic interludes between them as there had been in the past. While my mother hadn't possessed the strength in prior years to hold her own, she now repeatedly threw my father out as their fights, usually over money, grew more turbulent. She had also become increasingly distraught over her younger sister Lucy, who had continually chosen abusive men and given birth to too many of their children, and was currently checked into a mental hospital as my mother had been.

Aunt Lucy's new husband, our Uncle Ted, came by one day to discuss "the situation," but instead of appearing broken up over his wife's absence, he fawned over my mother, in a way my father hadn't in years. In her diminished physical state, and feeling the loss of her once-attractive self, the attention was like the joy of being handed her first-ever stick of cotton candy at the county fair. She lit up like a lamplight in the fog, slowly at first, then brighter as the mist dissipated. It wasn't long before he came over regularly, paying the kind of close attention to her—and to each of us kids—that made us squirm inside with unde-fined suspicion. When he and my mother started going into our room and shutting the door to be "alone," my mother saying she just wanted someone to talk to, our suspicion became outright anger for Gail and denial for me, as the sounds of their giggling and lovemaking escaped under the door.

At some point, Gail became so irate over the offensive syllables of their rendezvous that she burst into the bedroom.

"Get OUT," she screamed at Ted with the venom of a woman scorned. "I want you to get out!"

My mother scrambled to cover herself with the sheet and sat dumb-struck as Ted haphazardly threw his clothes on, practically tripping over his own feet to leave before Gail's verbal daggers slashed him to pieces beyond recognition.

But her intervention came too late.

My mother and Ted's not-so-clandestine routine—during which Uncle Ted had assured us that they were both going through difficult times and simply needed each other—had lasted long enough for my mother to soon bloom with the signature glow of pregnancy. Gail and I weren't strangers to what had made her belly expand once again, but I ardently continued to rebuff the obvious. It wasn't until my father found out, flinging strokes and spatters of crimson rage onto every surface of our living room, upending the coffee table and sending eve-rything on it flying like a fan of frightened birds, that we knew for a fact that the baby wasn't his.

———

That summer, while my mother caressed the vessel of her lover's child with a mixture of elation and sadness, I began spending more and more time with my maternal grandfather. A talented landscape architect, he would take me on jobs with him, introducing me to flowers and trees and the aesthetics of placing each element in its ideal growing space. He was the male role model I'd never had but always longed for. He also hated my father with a blackness that consumed him whenever he spoke of him, so much so that he once tried to kill him with a baseball bat for shirking his husband and father duties.

At that point, my father was so absent from my life that I felt nothing but detachment from him. But my grandfather was different. My grandmother had passed away after a long illness, and I had watched my grandpa care for her over the years in a way that touched me. He was gentle and kind, so when he invited me to sleep in his bed with him, I swelled with a feeling of much-longed-for connection.

Lying beside him, he pulled me close like a human cradle, the way a loving father would with a baby, my back touching his chest and stomach. I relished the feeling of his body next to mine, of his strong but caring arm around me. As we lay there snuggled together, talking about nothing and everything, I felt a comfort and sense of security beyond anything I'd ever experienced. But as I savored the pure bliss of our innocent bond, I noticed a growing stiffness against me. He said nothing, but I knew he was erect. He pulled me even closer, and we both fell asleep.

I spent several week-long visits with my grandfather that summer, each of which I craved with an unparalleled depth. At home, I would lie in the king-size bed I shared with my mother and sisters, feeling nothing akin to the adoration I felt in the arms of my grandfather. While my intuition whispered that his action was inappropriate—though he never did anything beyond holding me—I longed for our nighttime ritual of him pulling me close, believing with every fiber of my being that our intimacy was love.

———

Despite the scandalous circumstances, I eagerly awaited the birth of my mother's new baby. I felt certain the odds were with me and that it would be a boy, and I began to spend time in my makeshift airplanes imagining my little brother by my side, showing him the landscape from the vantage point of the heavens. I would pick flowers with him and teach him how to sneak into Gail's room to play Barbies. We would build tents and have picnics, and he would look up to me as I took his hand and made him my best friend.

When my mother went into labor, our Aunt Jane came to look after us. She seemed happy to be with us, but something about her demeanor was aloof, distracted. As I chattered on about how excited I was to have a brother, she merely looked at me and said, "You can't count on anything, Paul." I knew it was possible that my mother would bring home yet another sister, but I didn't expect her to come home with no baby at all.

Three days after my mother went into the hospital, she returned with swollen eyes and an air of deflation that curved her body into a compact version of herself, slowing her gait to a defeated shuffle. Heading straight for the couch, she collapsed onto it and reached for a cigarette, weakly ignited the match, then inhaled as if it were her life force and life extinguisher all at once.

The baby had been a boy.

And the baby had died.

I threw myself into my mother's lap and burst into tears. My brother, my perfect, brilliant, deeply loved brother would never know me, never fly with me, never hold my hand. *What happened?* we wanted to know through our sobs. My mother, in her attempt at consoling us, mumbled something about it being God's will.

I decided then and there that God must not grant wishes to eleven-year-old boys, no matter how badly they want them to come true.

And I wondered if my time spent snuggling with my grandfather had something to do with it.

CHAPTER ELEVEN

1965

Now in fifth grade, and with constant access to a few hundred bored kids ripe for entertainment, I poured my creativity into holding extravagant circus shows. I dragged refrigerator boxes from the dumpsters and borrowed shopping carts from a nearby store to construct a big top; I drew pictures of animals and clowns, and made signs in big letters that read COME ONE, COME ALL that I pinned to the cardboard. I was the obvious choice as the ringmaster, while Gail was the ticket-taker, Tina was our sideshow dancer, and Noel sold lemonade. I even trained a neighbor's dog to do tricks. We charged a nickel for admission, and another nickel for lemonade. Though everyone was poor, most could scrape together small change, and it added up to growing stashes for us kids. Plus, the cheering and clapping was a currency all its own.

One of the hardest things about living in poverty was the valiant endeavor to not wear it with a loudness everyone could hear. Though my mother, by what means I never knew with my father's limited support, always bought us nice outfits of high quality, there was a limit to how many she could afford. It didn't help that a wealthy neighborhood sat only a mile or two from the Village, and we had to attend school with dozens of kids whose armor shouted richness.

Obsessed since I was a toddler with how I looked, I simply couldn't bear wearing the same clothes over and over again. I knew it was useless to ask my mother to buy more, and my father barely showed his face at the complex, so I had no option but to earn my own money.

The circuses were one way to bring in an income, but it took a lot of effort for not a lot of revenue. So I scored myself a paper route. As my designated assistant, Tina would ride on the handlebars of my rickety bike and throw the papers onto the lawns of those I called out. I also babysat the young kids in the compound on a regular basis, sometimes spending four or five evenings a week in one of several equally miserable apartments.

With my earnings, which were substantial for a twelve-year-old, I bought only two things: clothes and shoes. Sure, I bought treats from time to time, but we usually snuck into movies through the back door and fetched uneaten candy from the garbage cans, so there was no need to waste money on sweets. It was wearables I cared about most, and I thoughtfully selected only the best I could afford. As a result, no one at school seemed to catch wind that I lived in the projects a short ride away.

Until I was hit by a car.

I was on my way home from school, no different from any other day, waiting at the corner of an intersection. After the light turned green, I stepped off the curb and onto the crosswalk. The next thing I felt was a crushing blow that sent me twenty feet into the air and fifty feet into the distance. When I came down on the asphalt, I skidded so fiercely on my back that I suffered a massive burn, not to mention a few broken bones and a concussion that felt like I had lost fifteen rounds of a prize fight. I remember scads of people rushing up to me, the sound of sirens, then nothing until I woke up in a hospital bed with my parents beside me.

"My baby, my baby," my mother cried, gently squeezing my hand.

"You're going to be okay," my father reassured me.

But feeling as if every organ and bone and tissue in my body was gasping to regain its breath, I couldn't imagine he was telling me the truth.

———

After a week, I was released from the hospital to recover in bed for a month. My teacher sent work home so I wouldn't fall further behind, and my mother pampered me with everything from soups to steak to sugary snacks. I was enjoying my slightly skewed Life of Riley, with my consistently fluffed pillows and chipper meal delivery, until a knock at our door shoved me off my pedestal.

My mother's voice wafted into my room as I heard her welcome visitors. I assumed they were kids from the complex, until a flock of opulent schoolmates appeared in the doorway.

"We heard what happened to ya," one boy said, "so we thought we'd come see how you were faring."

I stared at the five or so faces huddled together and saw how they were glancing around the room, some shifting uncomfortably, others looking at the floor. My heart contracted and expanded with the shame of my blown cover as I swallowed hard.

After a few awkward seconds passed, my friend Barbara said, "We brought you something." She stepped forward and set a fancy wrapped box on the bed. "The whole class chipped in."

My eyebrows danced chaotically on my forehead as I struggled to birth a coherent sentence.

"Thanks," I finally uttered. "That was awfully nice of you."

"Go on," someone said, hopping onto the bed. "Open your gift."

"Yeah, open your gift," the others chimed.

It took Herculean effort to steady my trembling hands, but I lifted the package and slowly tore off the paper. When I pried the lid from the box, a cobalt shirt with yellow polka dots, tucked inside a blue vest, smiled up at me.

My eyes grew wide. "What a swell gift!" I blurted out. I pulled the set from the tissue and held it up.

"We thought it was your style," Barbara said.

"It is," I nodded. "I love it!"

I saw the Bullock's tag, one of the finer stores of the day, dangling from the sleeve, and was touched by their generosity. Money may have been plentiful for most of them, but still.

A few more thorny moments leapt by, and then their questions began to fly.

"So, what happened?"

"Yeah, we heard the guy came out of nowhere."

"What was it like flying through the air?"

"Did you feel the pain when he hit you?"

"What was the hospital like?"

"Are you going to have a limp?"

"How long before you can come back to school?"

Before long, we had been engaged in lively conversation for half an hour, and I almost forgot that some of the wealthiest kids, including the daughter of a famous fast-food magnate, were sitting on the bed I shared with my mother and two sisters, the well-worn mattress moaning with every shift, discolored spots waving from the ceiling while smudges acted tough on the walls.

I almost forgot that in nearly every way, I didn't truly belong.

Almost.

———

After healing from the accident—but still carrying the utter mortification of having my classmates witness where I lived—I asked my mother if I could spruce up our apartment. My father, in his seemingly last act of forced generosity, had bought us some decent pieces of furniture for our living space, but I abhorred the sterile and stained white walls in every room. So, with my mother's blessing, I took the bills she slipped into my pocket and bought a few cans of paint in varied colors to jazz things up.

My mother loved the bursts of brightness that supplanted the previous glumness, but in all honesty, she was too consumed with her Al-Anon friends by then to notice a whole lot of anything. We had one telephone, and she was constantly on it, cradling the receiver between her cheek and shoulder as she lit up cigarette after cigarette, inhaling with an "I completely understand" or "You deserve so much better," then swishing the match out with two jerks of the wrist, tossing it into the ashtray as she tipped her head back, exhaling with an "I know just how you feel" or "You can't let him get away with that." It seemed every person within a ten-block radius knew my mother had been through the wringer with my father, and was therefore the most compassionate and understanding friend anyone could ask for. Being relied upon and respected—despite the fact that she had little respect for herself—got her through her own relapse of depression after the baby died, and she cherished every one of the lonely and battered souls who counted on her.

With my mother playing the role of counselor and confidante for hours on end to practically every woman in the group, my sisters and I became more and more self-sufficient. We also pretty much ran free in the complex with the other kids, gaining an appreciation of the pot-pourri of cultures in our backyard.

It was around this time that I began experimenting in the kitchen. I dragged out my mother's cookbooks and concocted items she'd never made, all of which were received with her enthusiastic applause.

"Oh honey, this is SO delicious," she would say, "SO much better than the things I make."

Seeing the pride on her face made losing my otherwise carefree time after school worth it, so I became our full-time cook. Anything I could do to alleviate burden from my mother's life was a balm for my soul. I had seen her suffer enough.

What I quickly discovered, however, was that as the month wound down, we had almost no food. I hadn't particularly noticed before that she made soups and stews near month's end, meals that could feed us all and stretch out for days. But now that I was largely in charge of food prep, I asked my mother for the money to replenish our stock.

"Your father abandoned us, Paul," she said curtly. "This is all we have until the first of the month, so you'll have to just make do."

I knew we were poor, and I knew my father was living his own version of the high life that didn't include us, but I hadn't realized *just* how strapped we were until then. So I learned to ration everything from butter to bread, making pastas, soups, and stews like my mother did that could feed our whole family for days.

I began to yearn with unrivaled angst for the arrival of the postman as the last day of the month dawned. I would rush home from school to snag the mail from the box, shuffling through it like a seasoned poker dealer to look for the welfare check and food stamps. Then, after practically forcing my mother to sign the check in the midst of one of her telephonic counseling sessions, I would both be desperate for and dread the trip to the store, where the shame of being on government assistance coated me like honey procured from holding bees at gunpoint. My eyes nervously scanned the aisles as we heaped canned goods and produce and boxed items and frozen meat into our cart, hopeful no kids from school were there, until we reached the checkout stand where I fidgeted and tapped my foot with my arms folded across my chest, looking anywhere but at my mother as she counted out the stamps like Monopoly money.

Once home from the market, I would plan the menus with the ingredients I had, then work hard to keep us from nearly starving by the time month's end rolled around.

My Aunt Jane, who often dropped in, poked her head into the kitchen one day and saw me stitching my brow together and making lists.

"What's he fretting about?" she asked my mother, hitching her thumb my way.

"Oh, he's taken on the job of cook." She paused, then whispered, "You know how it is."

Aunt Jane knew *exactly* how it was.

She took me by the arm and shuffled me into the living room, pushing the phone toward me with the demand that I call my father. "Tell him he needs to stop living like a bachelor and take care of his family, for God's sake!"

It was not the first time she forced me to call.

But it was one of the only times my father responded with cash instead of a rant and choice expletives.

It also marked the official demise of my childhood.

PART TWO

The Rendering

CHAPTER TWELVE

1968

The year I entered high school was the Dickensian "best of times and worst of times."

After decades of fighting for the equality and freedom that people of color should have never had to fight for in the first place, The Civil Rights Act was finally, triumphantly passed. Women were taking a stronger stand in society, and feminine independence was becoming more celebrated. Ann-Margret, Diahann Carroll, and Jane Fonda purred on the big and small screen; *Laugh-In* reinvented the variety show and introduced us to the delightfully dingy and scantily clad Goldie Hawn. Otis Redding watched the tide roll away "(Sittin' on) the Dock of the Bay" while Simon and Garfunkel implored Mrs. Robinson to hide her affair in the pantry with the cupcakes.

But amidst the victory and sexiness and evocative lyrics lay an undercurrent of uncertainty and fear over the shocking assassinations of Dr. Martin Luther King, Jr. and Senator Robert Kennedy, as well as artist Andy Warhol's narrow survival of the attempt on his life. Being a pacifist, I was deeply troubled by what I witnessed, but I was even more unsettled when the violent streak reached my typically passive mother.

My father had had multiple affairs while our parents were married, and all of us kids knew it. But it wasn't until he met Helen that he decided to separate from my mother and get his own place. He had lived there for years by this point, and Homewrecker Helen was there the majority of the time. We all resented her for breaking up our parents' marriage—though in hindsight there were plenty of other reasons—but I still stopped by on occasion to see him.

On this particular day, something possessed me to peek inside his bedroom window, which was very near the street. My mouth dropped open as I leaned closer and saw him having sex with Helen in broad daylight. I don't know why, but something in me snapped. Appalled, I took off running the few blocks home.

I bolted through the door and stopped hard at the couch.

"I just found Dad having sex with Helen," I said, my hands on my thighs as I heaved to catch my breath.

My mother's eyes grew wide. "What? Where?"

"In his . . . *breath* . . . bedroom . . . *breath* . . . through the window."

Suddenly, the same anger that had grabbed hold of me snatched my mother before my eyes. He could cheat, instigate nasty fights, move out, and give only intermittent financial support, but to know he was having sex with another woman at that very moment (no matter that he was in his own private bedroom), and that I had witnessed it, apparently gave my mother the long-time-in-coming excuse she needed to launch a confrontation. She abruptly stood up and strutted to the small bar top, took a couple hard swigs of whiskey, then called for my siblings.

"Come on, kids," she said, marching out the door.

"Where are we going, Mom?" Gail asked.

She swiped an errant strand from her forehead and tilted her head back. "I'm going to show that woman a thing or two."

"What woman?" Tina asked, sidestepping next to her.

My mother took a deep breath and held it as she replied, "Your father's girlfriend."

An incredulous look passed over my face. "You are?"

"Yep," she said, her determination fierce.

"What are you gonna do?" I wanted to know.

"You'll see."

She turned the corner with us trailing behind her, like the lead mallard followed by her obedient ducklings, and strode up to the door of my best friend's house. His mother was the woman I wished my once glamorous but now diminished mother could be: makeup done, fashionable outfits, a gorgeous face and figure with a bright smile for everyone.

My mother banged on the door. "Margaret!" *pause.* "MAR-GARET!"

My best friend's mother opened the door a crack. "Ramona?" she slurred. She glanced at us quickly. "What's going on?"

My mother bulldozed the door, sending Margaret a few teetering steps backward in her designer suit and spiked heels, her martini sloshing over the rim of the glass in one hand and ashes falling from her cigarette in the other. Her makeup was flawless as usual, with her hair swirled and set in all the right places, but she was clearly sauced. The glowing appearance I had revered was nothing more than a façade to hide that she was a blubbering drunk behind closed doors.

"Come on, Margaret," my mother said, grabbing her by the arm. "We've got work to do."

Margaret barely set her glass down before being whisked out the door and down the steps, seemingly too stunned to say a word. At fifteen, I was the prime age to be mortified accompanying my boozed-up mother and her hungover friend parading down the street, but I followed them just the same all the way to my father's house.

My mother told us to wait in the front yard as she busted in through the front door. Within minutes, she dragged poor Helen out of the house, my father fumbling with the zipper of his pants as he followed, and shoved her to the ground.

"Who do you think you are breaking up a marriage?" my mother seethed.

Helen jumped up with balled fists. "*I'm* not the one who broke up your marriage," Helen mocked, "*you* are."

My mother narrowed her eyes as our pounding hearts awaited the next move. "What did you say?"

"I said, '*you* are.'"

My mother's chest leapt then sank. My father yelled "Wait!" but it was too late. My mother rushed Helen and threw a punch at her. Helen kicked my mother in the shin, and Margaret kicked off her heels and dashed over to join in. Soon, all I saw was an abstract painting with smears of flailing limbs, jerking heads, and flying hair. My father stood like a statue in a macabre museum, uncertain what to do as we kids all cheered our mother on.

"Sock her!"

"Yeah, take her down!"

"Go for the gut, Mom!"

"Yeah, just like that!"

I had never seen women fight, and this one was epic: my mother and Margaret against the woman who symbolized every woman my father had chosen over his wife.

They punched and kicked, pulled hair and called each other demeaning names. Scratching whatever they could reach in the moment, they were down then up, then rolling on the grass, then grabbing a leg. Dresses were torn; shoes were strewn; Helen's prosthetic breasts, having been plucked out by my mother, lay embarrassed on the lawn.

Finally, after about ten minutes of mayhem (and no, my father didn't attempt to physically break it up), the fighting stopped. Our cheers became breathy sighs and an odd silence settled over us as Helen held a hand to her bloody mouth where my mother, completely crazed by uncharacteristic rage, had knocked out her front teeth. As I surveyed the chaotic scene, watching my mother and Margaret pant and brush the dirt from their clothes, I realized we had become *those* people, the ones who charge through the village with torches, determined to rid the town of the presumed bad seed, egging each other on in our hatred with every incensed proclamation to instill solidarity.

I felt some shame in that.

But seeing that level of resolve in my mother, who had been cloaked in fragility for so long that I assumed any layer of strength had long since been trampled, was something I would never forget.

It might have taken years, but the core of my mother's weakness died that day.

CHAPTER THIRTEEN

Throughout high school, I was fortunate to have numerous friends—both guys and girls. But there was one stark difference between us that I fought hard to keep a secret—the same one I concealed when we moved in the fifth grade—and that was where we lived.

It had been over four years at that point that we lived in Broadway Village. I had managed to hide it for the most part from my schoolmates, but it wasn't so easy now that I was in high school. Only a few blocks away, over the proverbial "tracks," dozens of ritzy houses glistened like castles in fairy tales; you could almost imagine that money really did grow on the trees in their yards. It was not only the neighborhood where most of my friends resided, it was also the one I had to walk through to get to school.

Wearing the designer clothes I loved—the ones I diligently earned working odd jobs—and that made me fit in with the rich kids, I would weave in and out of the streets, staring at the mansions, imagining what it would be like to live the lives of the people inside them. When I visited my friends, I was always in awe of the furnishings in their homes, their wardrobes, the cars they received for birthdays or Christmases like an expensive toy on their wish list. I had dreamed of a life like theirs since my childhood recesses spent fantasizing on the swings. So the shame of living in a known complex for low-income families was something that plagued me; in fact, I only trusted two guy friends with my actual address. So to avoid complete humiliation, I would always have my other friends drop me off after school or at night at the much more upscale complex called Broadway Royale. Waving them off, I would then walk the few blocks home. This went on until I graduated, with the excuse that my mother preferred I not bring friends home. This was a lie, of course—my mother loved my friends and wouldn't have minded in the least if I brought more home. But it was one of the many ways I struggled, and foundered, to live an authentic life, one that didn't involve pretending on some level that I was someone I wasn't.

During my mid-teen years, it was pretty much expected that popular guys date attractive girls. So being one of those people who resided on the unwritten popularity list, I regularly asked pretty girls out to preserve my reputation.

On a deep level—the one I buried and painted over with bravado—it was awkward; but in every other way, it was akin to the pure joy of playing with Gail's Barbie dolls as a boy. Although I was considered a "guy-guy," I relished being around girl energy. What's more, because I possessed a certain feminine relatability that most guys didn't, girls comfortably talked to me about everything, and they loved that I always noticed the details they cared about—their hair, their clothes, their nails, their makeup.

But while I honestly appreciated my girlfriends' beauty and enjoyed spending time with them as friends, by the time they wanted a more physical relationship, I would find some excuse—any excuse—to break up with them. I felt terrible doing it, but connecting intimately with a woman felt so unnatural to me that I simply couldn't bring myself to do it without feeling some level of repulsion. The few times one of my girlfriends kissed me, it took everything in me not to make her feel rejected. After we would split up, I would ask to stay friends, and happily for me, most of them obliged.

But none of them were as dear to me as Lynda.

A petite, bronze-skinned beauty with long, shiny chestnut hair worthy of a Breck commercial, Lynda was a gifted artist and my best friend. Her dad was a music manager who handled big-name groups and singers, so she was used to hanging out in a world of celebrities, parties, and fast living. She always carried a bottle of Jack Daniels or Southern Comfort with her, and she dabbled in various drugs on a regular basis.

One night, we were lying on the beach with no one around, smoking pot. As the inhibitions fell away, we started kissing, and my hand moved to caress her breast. She squirmed with pleasure, but something felt off. Even high, I could sense that I was trying to make a floral jacket go with plaid pants. They just didn't go together in anyone's definition of fashion. So while we didn't discuss it openly, she shrugged off my non-attraction to her with seeming understanding. She even slid effortlessly into being my "cover" date wherever we went, getting a kick out of the façade.

Lynda intrigued and excited me in an intellectual and artistic way. She was extremely well read, introducing to me to dystopian novels like *Brave New World* and *A Clockwork Orange*. She also represented everything I wanted to be as an artist. She possessed an evocative, contemporary style that depicted people and objects in a surrealistic way, the type of art you might find on an edgy album cover. She used painting to convey her imaginative interpretation of the world, and she encouraged me to do the same. So I began drawing and painting more often, reveling in how aligned I felt. I even wondered if it might be possible to one day make a living as an artist. But I had been poor my entire childhood, and I knew that the term "starving artist" wasn't an exaggeration. So I put aside the notion of becoming an artist professionally; I wanted the grand lifestyle I had always dreamed of: living in a beautiful home, running freely on the beach, driving fancy cars, and wearing the finest clothes. I wanted my house to be open and modern, splashed in a combination of calming blues and greens and exhilarating reds and oranges, with the kind of fine furniture that exuded both ritziness and comfort, not a putty-walled, cereal-box-sized apartment filled with hand-me-downs, childhood remnants, and thrift-store bargains. I wanted rugs in alternating and complementary patterns to cushion the tables, couches, and chairs, and I wanted museum art to pop on the walls, some of which might be my own, attracting thoughtful interpretation and conversation. I wanted to have numerous wide, tall windows facing the ocean, where I could watch the tide ebb and flow and hear the waves crash gently on the shore, lulling me to sleep in my luxurious bed and linens. And inside an enormous closet, I envisioned having a bevy of pressed designer shirts in varying colors and prints lining an entire wall, with equally stylish jeans and pants accompanying them, and rows and rows of trendy shoes in browns, blacks, tans, and navy standing proudly in their wooden racks. Only in my free time would I enclose myself in my contemporary, high-ceilinged studio, with plenty of space for creative expression, surrounded by scores of canvases and easels, and tables filled with paints and brushes, with just the right light pouring in, where the walls and floor would gain character as I splattered paint with abandon to shape my original creations. One collection might hang in a gallery; other pieces might sell to interested buyers, supplementing my already ample income. I didn't want to ever worry again about making groceries last till month's end—I wanted to eat in fancy restaurants, or make lovely meals at home and serve them on beautiful dishes. And it wasn't just for me that I wanted these things. I wanted to give my mother everything she had lacked—a lovely home, pretty clothes, elegant meals out. I wanted to host frequent parties for laughing, beaming friends, sprint with them down the shoreline and swim with them in the ocean, and ensure they felt welcome and at home—not enveloped by a sense of pretense or pompousness—in my opulent surroundings.

And I didn't see any of that happening unless I pursued a lucrative career outside the art world.

But I almost didn't live to find out.

Outside my high school friends, I hung out with my offbeat posse in Broadway Village, one of whom was a cool girl named Zoma who was a few years older than me. Beautiful in a dark, Gothic way, she slinked through the neighborhood in her signature long, black velvet cape, bringing stark attention to her smooth ivory complexion and contrasting crimson lipstick. Her indifference—and frequent drug use—had gotten her sent to reform school (which made her even cooler in the adolescent world); depending on her drug of choice, she wasn't always completely "there," but I loved spending time with her.

When Zoma moved, her absence stung; I missed our nights of lying low, listening to music and being hippies together. So one night, my friend Charlie and I decided to hitchhike to Zoma's new place.

After a few minutes of thumbing it on the side of the road, a guy with ratty hair and a crinkly leather jacket slowed to a stop and rolled down the passenger window. "Where're you two headed?"

I bent down to his eye level. "Not far. Just a friend's house a few miles from here."

The guy looked us over in a strange, leering way, then said, "Okay, hop in."

We had no sooner climbed into the backseat when the guy took off like a bullet. He cranked the music and craned his neck toward us. "Howz about I deliver you and your friend in a box?" he shouted.

Charlie and I looked at each other as we careened down the road, wondering if we should be scared or merely creeped out by his comment. But it quickly became clear, as we recklessly swerved block after block under the driver's maniacal laugh, that the guy was more than just creepy.

"Hey! Slow down!" Charlie said repeatedly.

But the driver was like a man possessed. As soon as he had the chance, he gunned it full speed toward a pole. With no chance of saving us, we crouched down just before impact. Glass shattered like a sharp-edged snowfall as Charlie and I were thrown hard into the back of the front seats. The sound of crunching metal pierced the air and seemed to compress us as steam began hissing from the front like a pit of snakes.

"Holy shit!" Charlie said. "What the fuck just happened?" He moaned as he tried to turn toward me. "You okay?"

I lifted my head slowly. "I guess," I said, rubbing my neck. "But oh my god, what a fucking lunatic!"

"I know! The asshole tried to kill us!"

I pulled myself painfully into a sitting position and peered into the front seat. The driver was slumped in a disturbingly twisted way onto the steering wheel and blood was everywhere. "He doesn't look good," I said to Charlie.

"You think he's dead?"

"Looks like it. We better get out of here before the car blows."

Charlie eased his way up, wincing. "Yeah," he agreed.

Despite having multiple lacerations and aching from head to toe, we forced the back doors open and punched them out with our feet.

When we tumbled out, we found ourselves smack in front of Forest Lawn Cemetery. *What are the odds?* I thought. We managed with pure adrenaline to climb the cemetery wall and scramble up a nearby hill. Miraculously, we seemed to escape with no major injuries.

Before long, sirens and swirling red lights splattered us with an unmerited sense of guilt as we crouched in the dark under a tree.

"Should we talk to the cops?" Charlie asked.

"Hell, no. And get busted for hitchhiking? We don't want to be associated with that creep."

"I guess."

Our bodies pulsed with pain like bubbles in a hot spring as we cowered in the shadows of the moonlight, watching the scene on the street below.

It took at least half an hour, but firefighters finally pried the guy out. Within minutes, paramedics zipped him into a body bag, his apparent death wish fulfilled.

Those punched-out doors were surely evidence that the driver wasn't alone, but no one ever found out it was us who had been in the car.

In the days that followed, I found it difficult to stop trembling. I had been in the second serious accident in my young life, and I couldn't help but wonder why. Was it a giant lesson not to hitchhike because next time it could be worse? Was I damned for the way I felt toward men? Or was it a message that I had a bigger purpose, and because I survived, I'd better not squander it? I obviously favored that one, only at seventeen, I didn't know what my purpose was. It crossed my mind that perhaps it was related to art, but I still wasn't interested in trying to make a career of it, eating cold beans out of cans with plastic spoons six nights a week, living out of a dented Volkswagen Bus, my only privacy provided by a set of homemade calico curtains.

———

Not long after the accident, I went over to my friend Mike's one night. His family owned a motel, and Mike had his very own hippie pad next door where a bunch of the cool kids hung out on a regular basis.

When I arrived, Marvin Gaye's "What's Goin' On" floated through the foggy space and lava lamp blobs cast eerie shadows on the low-lit walls. Someone stuck a beer can in my hand, and I collapsed into an empty beanbag chair where I could see everyone smoking and snorting and drinking their way into enlightenment. One by one, guys disappeared with girls into another room to have quick sex, then returned with loopy smiles and mussed hair.

Another beer.

Then someone changed the album to Simon and Garfunkel.

Like a bridge over troubled water
I will lay me down . . .

Another beer and couple more songs.

Oh, Cecilia, I'm down on my knees
I'm begging you please to come home . . .

Another beer and a couple more songs.

I am just a poor boy
Though my story's seldom told . . .

Another beer and a couple more songs.

Hey, I've got nothing to do today but smile
Da-n-do-da-n-do-da-n-do here I am . . .

"It's your turn, Paul," someone finally said, raising a bottle of tequila my way.

A pretty girl climbed onto my lap and invited me with a sultry beckoning of her index finger to take her away. I flirted with her briefly, then eased her off my lap. I had no plans to have sex with any girl and decided it was probably time that I leave.

Bye bye love, bye bye sweet caress
Hello emptiness, I feel like I could di-ie . . .

I was easing my way up and out of the beanbag chair when dizziness hit me like I had just gotten off the Tilt-a-Whirl. Trying to get my balance, I stumbled toward a plate-glass door and heard a crash. When I narrowed my eyes to see where the sound came from, I saw that my arm had broken through the glass—and that my right hand was hanging from my wrist, almost completely severed.

"Oh my god," a girl shrieked. "His hand's chopped off!"

Despite being stoned and drunk, a few people rushed to me. All at once, I saw their eyes enlarge like just-clicked-on headlights.

"Holy shit!" a guy said. "Look at all that blood!"

"Jesus," Mike said. "That's bad. Really bad."

I had never been one to do anything in excess, but something had propelled me that night to down a six-pack within a two-hour period, and I'd smoked part of a joint too, leaving me feeling no pain. "Christ," I slurred, afraid to move. "I can't lose my hand."

But we couldn't call an ambulance. We were all underage and would go to jail for sure. And no one was in any state to drive. So a few moderately with-it friends eased my arm back through the shards, cradling my near-detached hand, then wrapped my wrist tightly in a T-shirt and tied it off.

I don't remember how exactly I ended up in the ER, or what I said to the nurses. All I know is, some angel was watching over me. Clearly, I was drunk and couldn't pretend I wasn't; but perhaps because I was so severely injured, everyone looked the other way.

Everyone, that is, except for my mother and the doctor assigned to me.

When my mother arrived she was visibly upset, not only because I needed extensive surgery to save my hand, but because I was being uncharacteristically obnoxious, swearing loudly and making a scene. The doctor, trying to keep me from being hauled off to a cold cell after I recovered from surgery, took my mother by the arm and leaned in close.

"You know," he said, "we're obligated to call these cases in to the police. When they arrive, he'd better not be acting like this. I think it's best if I give him a sedative."

My mother nodded in understanding, then hovered close to my face.

"Paul," she whispered coarsely. "You need to be quiet or you're going to get arrested. The doctor's going to give you something to knock you out, okay?"

I blinked hard as her tired eyes came into focus. I saw the way she was looking at me, with that deep worry I wanted so much to save her from.

"Okay," I nodded. "I'm sorry." Then I closed my eyes and felt myself drift off.

———

When I woke up from surgery, sober but groggy, I looked down at the massive club of bandages that was now my right arm. *Jesus*, I thought. *What have I done?* That's when it hit me hard: any chance of being an artist had likely just ended. I had nearly died twice and survived, and for what?

I may have been adamant about avoiding the lifestyle of a starving artist, but at that moment, I promised God and myself that if I was ever able to use my hand again, I wouldn't waste my gift.

If, I thought, *I'm not damned the way I fear.*

CHAPTER FOURTEEN

It took months to recover the use of it, but by some miracle, I regained full motion of my right hand. Wanting to grab life by the reins, I vowed to stay away from drugs and alcohol, and I decided to do everything I could to graduate early.

Being a year older than everyone in my grade, I had mostly hung out with Gail's friends, and they had all graduated. Besides, Gail had never been keen on her little brother being latched on to her group. In fact, she once asked her boyfriend to "get rid of me," and he took it literally—twisting my arm behind my back so severely that he broke my humerus. I had not only grown tired of having to recover from major injuries, but I was also tired of feeling like the odd guy out. So although I made a new group of artsy, Bohemian friends as a senior, I signed up for zero period and extra credit to finish a semester early.

My before-school class was taught by a handsome man named Greg. I was the only one in the class, and it wasn't long before Greg started walking up to my desk and putting his hand on my shoulder while he talked to me, or sitting across from me with a twinkle in his eye. I had never had a guy be openly flirtatious with me before, so despite the fact that he was ten years older and married, I flirted back. This went on for a few weeks until one day, he invited me to come to his house after school.

I met him in the faculty parking lot and we silently drove to his beach pad. He saw me looking around anxiously as we pulled into his driveway.

"My wife's not home," he said. "So don't worry."

I let out a breath. "Okay." Which came out with a slight lilt at the end like a question.

I didn't know what his intentions were, but I knew that the excitement I felt being with this man, at his house alone, was almost more than I could handle. As a teacher, I knew he was taking a huge chance; as a student, I was too. But the buildup from weeks of flirtation to this moment made all that feel irrelevant.

"Come on in," he said. He tossed his keys into a glass dish, making me jump. "Don't be nervous," he laughed.

"I'm not," I lied, shrugging it off nonchalantly.

As I meandered into the living room, I noticed the photos on the mantle, one of which was of the bride and groom. A wedding photo staring at me wasn't what I had in mind, but I didn't know *what* I had in mind, so I stood there waiting for Greg to make the first move.

"Let's go outside," he said. "We should be getting a beautiful sunset soon."

He motioned toward the French doors and led me out back to a huge cluster of rocks overlooking the ocean.

He tilted his head up and to the left. "There's a great spot right over here."

I followed him along the jagged path, hoping he couldn't hear my heart beating as I sat down beside him.

"Isn't this gorgeous?" he said, looking out to the horizon.

"It is," I agreed. "There's nothing I love more than the ocean."

He turned to me and began caressing my leg. "I have such a crush on you."

"You do?" I said, feeling my cheeks flush.

"Uh huh. I've been dying to get you off that campus."

"Really?"

He nodded and licked his lips seductively. Then he leaned in slowly and put his sensuous mouth on mine. My body surged with adrenaline as I kissed him, then the testosterone flowed straight to my groin as he put his hand on my crotch. His tongue roamed my mouth as the sensations of what sex with the right person could feel like flooded my entire being.

As I was reveling in my first male kiss, a pang of doubt shot through me. I couldn't help but wonder what Greg was doing with me. I was young; he was married. I didn't want to stop, but I didn't know where the relationship could possibly go. I pulled away gently.

"What's wrong?" he asked.

"Nothing . . . it's just that . . . I feel weird being here when I know you're married."

He smiled as if comforting a child. "Oh honey, my wife and I have an understanding."

I glanced away for a moment and pondered his answer. It wasn't a perfect solution, but I couldn't reject the cravings I had to kiss him some more.

"Okay, then," I said tentatively. Then we pulled each other close and resumed where we left off.

Greg invited me to his home on two more occasions, where we kissed passionately and let our hands freely roam each other's bodies. I was overwhelmed by how natural it felt for me to be with a man in a physical way, and despite the less-than-ideal circumstances, I wondered when or if we might take our intimacy to the next level.

But he didn't want to jeopardize his teaching career, though I wasn't sure how anyone could ever know what we did in his home, so we never did more than kiss and touch. I also think he believed he wasn't really cheating if our time together didn't escalate to sex. So this "affair-light" secretly continued, remaining mostly innocent experimentation.

But Greg wasn't the only teacher who flirted with me.

Jim was a brilliant artist and photographer, and he was head of our school's art department. Being in the art program, I saw him a lot and we developed a friendship. But just like Greg, Jim only kept his feelings to himself for so long before he began flirting with me on the sly. While we never connected on an intimate level and were careful on campus to never be seen together outside the art department, there was no denying the testosterone surges we both felt in each other's presence. There was also no denying my compounding confusion.

———

After my innocent fling with Greg, and Jim's obvious attraction to me and mine to him, I became obsessed with the sexual urges I had, knowing I was compatible with men. But I was also extremely ashamed of it. So despite lying awake at night, envisioning living in a new place with a wonderful man with whom I could live freely, I strove ardently to hide my feelings and emotions from my family and most of my long-term friends.

Although the tides were changing, and for most people the sixties was a time of sexual awakening and experimentation, being visibly gay was still highly frowned on by society. In fact, loving the wrong person could make you a criminal. Something as innocuous as a man smiling at another man in the park, taken the wrong way, could lead to arrest; being found in a gay man's address book could cost you a prison sentence. Hundreds of thousands of men feared being picked up by zealous police hungry for easy convictions, often for doing nothing more than "looking" a bit gay.

But it was 1971, and it would be decades before the US Supreme Court ruled, in Lawrence v. Texas, that intimate consensual sexual conduct was part of the liberty protected under the Fourteenth Amendment. So I cloaked my true sexuality in darkness and acted as "straight" as I could—with everyone except for Lynda.

Lynda knew I wasn't attracted to women, and she was hip to alternative lifestyles, so she willingly fed my more adventurous side. One night, she drove me to a gay nightclub she knew of several miles from Broadway Village. I wasn't of age to go in, so we just hung out for hours in the parking lot, knocking back some of her always-on-hand Jack Daniels or Southern Comfort, getting mildly high and listening to music, rating the guys as they came and went. The excitement of what became a weekend ritual was akin to knowing as a child that you were going to Disneyland on Saturday and had the whole week to look forward to it.

The mere idea of being near so many gay men made my body pulse with adrenaline. At the same time, I was plagued with the belief of how "wrong" most everyone said it was to feel the way I did. People were constantly throwing ugly words at homosexuals—faggot, freak, abomination, sinner. I didn't understand how God could make me the way he did and then want me to suffer and be ostracized, especially by clergy and the ultra-religious, people who were supposed to embrace love above all. But growing up in the Catholic Church had driven home the image of a vengeful God we were supposed to fear—which gave no comfort to a young man who was told it was wrong to be who he was, while it felt equally wrong to try to be someone else.

So the nights Lynda and I spent as voyeurs in the parking lot of the nightclub struck the balance between allowing myself to feel my natural attraction to men without actually doing anything that might get me arrested.

Until I spotted Dan.

He was striding across the lot toward his car, and his striking good looks captured my attention like the sun beaming unexpectedly through a storm cloud–riddled sky. I was immediately drawn to him, but I was too shy to jump out of the car to say hi. So when we came back the next weekend, Lynda and I hung around outside as it got later, hopeful that he would be there.

After several hours, the door to the club swung open and out walked Dan.

"Go on," Lynda whispered, "this is your chance!"

I hurried my steps without running until I caught up with him. "Hi," I said. "I'm Paul."

He turned, almost startled, then his face melted into a warm smile. "Well hello, Paul," he said, raising his eyebrows. "I didn't see you inside." He looked me up and down as my heart marched with a vengeance. "You're cute. But you're young, aren't you?"

I was grateful that the lampposts cast a shadow over my flushed face. "I guess . . . I'm eighteen."

Dan nodded seductively. "Well that may be too young to get into the club, but it's not too young to have some fun."

I could feel the blood racing through my body, but I was also scared. Anyone could be a plant, so I played straight.

"What kind of fun?" I asked.

"Well, you're here in the parking lot of a gay nightclub, so I assume you're looking for sex."

"No, no," I said adamantly. "Not sex. Maybe we could . . . just hang out as friends."

He gave me another once-over, then threw a couple of eyebrow somersaults my way as if playing along. "Sure, we can be friends, if that's what you want."

Over the next couple weeks, Dan and I met for coffee a few times, with Lynda tagging along playing the role of my girlfriend. We would stay out until the wee hours of the morning, the time melting away as the three of us talked.

Mesmerized by Dan's stunning blue eyes, chiseled jaw, and overwhelming sexiness, as well as impressed by his job as the manager of a Standard shoe store—which was a huge, well-known company—I had to constantly remind myself that I was "with" Lynda. I don't know how long he bought my charade, especially since it was impossible to hide that we were both attracted to each other, but to his credit, he went along with my declaration of being straight.

The fourth time we met, Lynda didn't tag along, and Dan suggested that we go to his apartment where we would "be more comfortable." Flooded with excitement at the thought of being alone with him, I agreed.

When we arrived, my mouth dropped open. His apartment was exactly what I dreamed of for myself. The walls were a cool blue, the perfect backdrop to set off the mahogany and walnut furniture that sank into his plush cream carpeting. The windows were wide and offered a great view, and every surface was peppered with classy objects: vintage flea market finds, various types of candles, leather-bound books, expensive sculptures.

"Your place is gorgeous," I exclaimed, unable to contain my admiration.

"Thanks," he called over his shoulder as he headed into the kitchen. "Can I get you something? A drink, maybe?"

"No, thanks," I said, wanting to stay completely sober in the moment. "I'm fine."

He returned to the living room with a glass of something he set on the coffee table. He struck a match and lit some pillar candles, then flicked on the turntable and set the needle down on an Al Green album.

When he turned around, his collection of stunning features, combined with the smooth melody of the music, made me tremble like I was in the presence of an idol.

"You want to see my shoe collection?" he asked.

"Sure," I said a bit too eagerly, feeling a bit like a kid whose dad just asked if he wanted to go to work with him that day.

"Come on," he motioned, leading me to his bedroom.

He flipped on the light in his closet and there stood three tall racks of shoes, all resting perfectly in their assigned cubbies, color-coded and arranged by style.

"Wow," I said. "This is exactly what I'd like to have someday."

"Well, I'm sure you will," he said, taking my hand. He placed his palm against mine and stretched out his fingers. A bolt of electricity shot through me. All of my prior fantasies of being with men reached an apex in that moment. He wasn't married, and he wasn't one of my teachers, making him the first real candidate for a relationship I had ever had. I knew he was probably five or six years older than me, but in that stirring pocket of time, with his hand pressing against mine, I didn't feel like a high school kid, and I got the feeling he didn't see me as one either.

"Shall we leave the closet?" he asked with a wink.

I chuckled at the double entendre. "Sure."

He brought our hands down together in a slow, sweeping motion and led me into his bedroom. He faced me and immediately put his mouth gently on mine, kissing me with an intensity that overwhelmed me, as he ran his hand up and down my back. I pulled him close to me, every inch of my body yearning for him to touch me. He seemed to get the message because he pulled off my shirt and unbuttoned my pants, and I did the same to him, kissing passionately between each removal of a sleeve and easing out of a leg, before collapsing onto his bed in a whirlwind of intimacy that lasted for hours.

After my first sexual encounter with Dan, he was all I could think of. In fact, it was all I could do to concentrate on school and stick to my plan of graduating early. Because I couldn't go to any nightclubs or bars with him, we had to spend the majority of our time together at his apartment; neither one of us wanted to risk being out too much in public, not with the attraction we felt to each other that was too intense to be ignored.

At that point in my life, I pretty much did as I pleased. My mother tried but failed to enforce a curfew, and she wasn't terribly nosy about where I spent my evenings out, so I began spending the night at Dan's. After a few weeks, he asked if I wanted to move in with him, and I didn't hesitate for a moment to say yes.

Although I still had a couple months of high school to finish, I moved my meager belongings into Dan's luxury pad and felt as if I had just won the lottery. Dan was gorgeous, built, and successful, and he was in love with me. We shared a closeness and compatibility that was instant, and I couldn't imagine feeling anything but deeply in love with him.

I had no idea how much a person could hide in the vortex of wild, consuming sex and burgeoning love.

CHAPTER FIFTEEN

After graduating in December, I eased into living an essentially adult married life. Dan worked days at the store while I took courses at the junior college nearby, and at night, after I spent my requisite time studying, we curled up in his apartment, playing Motown records and making passionate love. When I was home alone before classes, I would admire all the clothes in Dan's closet, noting the stylish way he put certain outfits together, and follow his lead as he added to my wardrobe. He looked so cool the way he inhaled his cigarettes, then tipped his curly blonde head back to exhale, that I took up smoking too. With my newly acquired fake ID, we went to clubs together on weekends, where he proudly introduced me as his sweetheart to all his friends, and I was warmly welcomed into their circles.

In the initial two years of our relationship, I felt like the happiest, most liberated person alive. For the first time, I was living a semi-authentic life, sharing it with someone I loved deeply and who I believed loved me equally. I had always longed for a loving, stable, committed relationship, and Dan provided all those things, along with a beautiful place to call home. Even my mother fell in love with him. Although he and I lived together under the guise of being roommates, and my mother never brought up the possibility that it was more, she quickly embraced him as her other son, and he developed a genuine closeness with her. He came to love her as his second mother and treated her like a queen, which endeared him to me even more.

In addition to being my best friend and lover, Dan supported me financially, paying for my tuition, books, and art supplies. While I sincerely appreciated his generosity, and he always offered it willingly, it gave me some degree of guilt that he spent his hard-earned money on my education. Although college helped me gain maturity and discipline, and I became more punctual and organized, I continued to struggle with what was likely undiagnosed ADD. Fearing I simply wasn't smart enough in certain courses to achieve decent grades on my own, I frequently cheated to get them. I hated being dishonest and the worry of getting caught by one of my professors, but Dan and my mother were so proud of my accomplishments that I simply couldn't allow anything to tarnish their opinion of me. At that time in my life, nothing meant more to me than their approval.

————

After Dan and I had been together for a couple of years, and I had transferred to the university as an art major, I came home from school one evening to find him propped on the couch like a plank, his neck cradled against the back and his body sloping down, a drink in his hand, his eyes peering downward toward me under heavy lids. I was used to him drinking casually, but he knew how I felt about alcohol abuse—I had seen what it did to my father, not to mention the three hundred stitches it took to reattach the arteries of my right wrist—so he had mostly respected my desire to stay sober. On this night, however, something had caused him to abandon that agreement.

"Where've you been?" he asked accusingly.

I pulled back, alarmed by his tone. "What do you mean? You know I've been at school."

"Have you?" he said, raising a cynical brow. "How do I know you weren't off with that teacher you had a thing for in high school?"

My face fell. "What? You mean Greg?"

He stayed quiet but glared at me.

"Oh please. You know that was an innocent fling a long time ago." I tried to laugh it off. "Why would you even ask that?"

He remained eerily still. "How do I know what you do when you say you're at school? For all I know, you could be having an affair with one of your professors."

My mouth dropped as I squeezed my eyes shut then reopened them. "What are you talking about? I've never been unfaithful to you. You know that." He rolled his eyes toward the ceiling as I tossed my jacket on a chair. "Where is this coming from?"

He sat up slowly and set his drink on the table. "You think I don't see how other men look at you?"

I deflected his comment with a sarcastic grin. "No different from how they look at you."

At that, he bolted up and was immediately in front of me. He grabbed me by the arms. "Uh-uh. You're not going to make this about me."

I retreated and looked away, frightened by his uncharacteristic aggression. A few awkward moments passed, then he suddenly softened and pulled me to him. He wrapped his arms around my back so tightly that I felt nearly suffocated and deeply treasured at the same time.

"It's just that you're my everything," he said, his voice tight.

I hugged him back and laid my head against his chest. "You're my everything too."

———

Not long after Dan's latent jealousy began popping up like a jack-in-the-box, then stuffed again and again into its temporary hiding place after nights of intense passion, I was putting laundry away when I found a bag of cocaine in his sock drawer. I had never seen him snort coke before, and I wondered how long he'd had it. But his unreliable behavior lately had me a little on edge, so I was hesitant to ask.

When he came home from work in a chipper mood, I decided to toss the subject out nonchalantly, so as not to put him too much on the defensive. Setting our dinner on the coffee table, I said, "Hey, I found this today putting your socks away." I pulled the bag out of my pocket and dropped it next to his dish.

He glanced at it with no expression. "Yeah. So?"

"So . . . since when do you do coke?"

"Since I felt like it."

I sighed. "Why, Dan?"

He shrugged. "What difference does it make? You're no saint."

Offended by his tone, but playing it cool, I said, "Pot's not a big deal. But coke? It's just kind of intense, don't you think?"

I could sense by the look on his face that he resented my opinion.

"You can't tell me what to do," he sneered with a flick of his hand as he clicked on the remote. "Now let's eat."

———

Over the next several months, the gentle rolling waves of Dan's and my blissful existence became a veritable storm that swelled and calmed without warning. Along with unmerited jealousy and a voracious appetite for sex that drove him to cheat on me with other men, Dan's growing addiction to alcohol and drugs made him radical and unpredictable. He still professed his love for me, however, and our passion was as strong as ever, so I held fast to the good times and dealt the best I could with the rest.

But there was no denying that Dan was hurting me deeply with his actions. He had no reason to mistrust me, yet he repeatedly blamed me for his affairs; the more drugs he did, the more paranoid he became. So, while I had no desire to be unfaithful, I felt that if I received attention from other men, it would fill the growing void inside me. I also stupidly assumed that I would feel some satisfaction in playing Dan's game.

So I called Greg. He was still married and teaching at my high school. He was also happy to hear from me. I hated the idea of using him to get back at Dan, but I agreed to see him anyway.

Greg and I began a short affair, which consisted of whirlwind meetings and unsatisfying sex, but a part of me allowed it to be a balm on my wounded ego. Each time I showed up at Greg's house, I wondered how long the fling would last. But I didn't have to wonder for long.

One afternoon, as our kissing was escalating toward a full sexual encounter, Greg's wife came home early and found us half dressed in the living room. It would be an understatement to say that she lost it; there was clearly no "understanding" between them for extramarital dalliances, especially not with men.

"What the hell is this, Greg?! Who is this kid and what are you doing with him?"

Greg stammered. "We were . . . just playing around . . . nothing serious."

"Not serious, my ass!" she said, grabbing my shirt from the floor and throwing it at me. "You were about to have sex right here on my couch, weren't you?"

I punched my arms through my sleeves and hurriedly fastened the buttons.

"Get OUT!" she demanded, seething at me.

Greg stood up and reached out to touch her arm, but she yanked it away.

"Babe, don't take it out on him," he attempted in a calm voice. "He's just a friend."

"Seriously, Greg? You think I'm going to buy that? Give me a fucking break!"

I slipped on my shoes and didn't wait for Greg to protest. I dashed past them and out the door, then drove home to find Dan singing to a Supremes album while he cooked me a three-course apology dinner for the way he'd been acting.

———

In the weeks that followed, the apology dinner quickly digested and forgotten, Dan continued his erratic behavior—and I continued to cheat to get back at him. Several of my professors in the art department had flirted with me, and until then, I had pretended not to notice. But now, with Dan's insatiable appetite for sex being fulfilled by any number of men other than me, I embraced the flattery of my professors with newfound resolve; because I looked up to them and respected them, I surmised that if an intelligent, confident, talented man wanted me, then I must be pretty special.

But just like with Greg, the sex was never satisfying; it only served to paint my insides with the darkest shade of shame. I wondered if, sex aside, I was merely looking for a father figure with these older men. But I reasoned that it wasn't about age or these men loving me like a son; it was more about the male attention and mentoring I received from these highly educated professionals that drew me to them. The problem was, Dan's and my now-dysfunctional relationship had immersed me in a consuming pool of confusion. I was young and he was my first love. I couldn't imagine leaving him, yet I also couldn't imagine allowing him to be unfaithful with my knowledge and do nothing.

Caught up in the fire and ice of our fights and lovemaking as if they had become mutually exclusive, I became someone I never wanted or intended to be: a person who adopted and submitted to an abusive relationship. I hated how rotten it made me feel, but the love and passion were still as present as ever, so I stayed. Had Dan pushed me away both emotionally and physically, even after I threw in his face several times that I was cheating too, it might have been different. But every time he held me close and kissed me, or bought a beautiful gift for my mother, or made me a romantic dinner followed by hours of consuming intimacy, whatever anger we harbored melted away.

But the truth was that despite our redeeming physical connection, I was constantly troubled by the fact that Dan's values and morals were not in sync with my own, and that I had compromised mine in a futile effort to hold on to him. I was ashamed that I had used my professors and our mutual friends to lash out at him, and I felt myself growing away from him each time I attempted to turn a blind eye to his lies and infidelities. Yet somewhere inside me, I clung to the misguided notion that I could—and would—change him. It was the biggest misconception I entertained, and the greatest lesson I would learn: that a person, no matter the depth of love he may have for you, can only change for himself.

———

After another year of living in a never-ending hopscotch game, where each square represented some hot or cold aspect of Dan's and my un-healthy relationship, I felt more empty than ever. I had started working at a famous, world-class hotel as a bellman, and I was still going to school during the day, so in some ways I was lucky that I was too busy most of the time to know what Dan was up to.

Soon after I started working at the hotel, a businessman I escorted to his room reached into his pocket to give me a tip. But instead of the usual five dollar bill, he handed me a fifty.

"Will this be enough for you to score me a hooker?"

My eyes grew wide. "A hooker?"

"Yeah. You must know everything that goes on around here. Can you get me a pretty one?"

I squirmed slightly in my bellman suit, yet the weight of the fifty in my hand swayed me. "Sure. I guess so."

"Great," he said, loosening his tie. "I'll be waiting."

With that, I wheeled the luggage cart into the elevator and won-dered what I had just gotten myself into.

After what I thought would be a one-time proposition, other busi-nessmen began to ask me to score them prostitutes as well, offering me anything from fifties to hundreds. Though I was never a fan of women denigrating themselves for money, and I knew getting caught could lose me my job, the big tips were hard to refuse. Plus, I figured it was none of my business.

But not long after, the proposition shifted.

One evening, I put a small set of expensive luggage on the cart and took a handsome businessman in his pressed suit up to his room.

"Will there be anything else, sir?" I asked.

He stared at me provocatively and smiled. "If you're willing."

I assumed I'd be asked to find yet another hooker. "Sure," I said.

"You up for a little playing around?" he asked.

"Me?"

"Yes, you. You like men, don't you?"

For all the effort I made to never appear gay to anyone, this assumption unnerved me. But it also flattered me. Caught in the awkward moment, my mind flashed the reasons I shouldn't do it. *He's a stranger. I'm with Dan. I'm not a male escort. This isn't me.* Then I thought, *He finds me attractive. Dan's cheating anyway. He'll probably offer me a nice sum of money. I can buy my mom something nice with that money.*

"Okay," I finally said. Then I swallowed and added, "For three hundred."

"Done," the guy said.

I tried not to let my expression belie my surprise. "Okay. My shift ends in about an hour. I'll meet you here then?"

He smiled. "I'll look forward to it."

That night, and subsequent nights with other well-to-do men who hid behind briefcases and wedding bands, I accepted this "gay for pay" arrangement for a brief time, though it went against everything I believed in. The reasoning may have been skewed, but I honestly wanted the extra money so that I could at long last pamper my mother, buying her some nice new clothes and taking her to fancy restaurants with money that was mine, not Dan's. Had she known how I earned it, she would have been mortified. What's more, my reluctant promiscuity that led to sexual intimacy was never fulfilling in the way it was with Dan, and though I was smitten a few times, I never became emotionally invested with any of the men I spent time with.

Feeling emotionally and spiritually bankrupt, I turned to the one person I felt I could talk to: my father's new wife.

When I was a sophomore in high school, my dad met Shirley, a classy Zsa Zsa Gabor-type who was a school psychologist. Despite his drinking and transparent charm, Shirley, with her platinum blonde hair and stylish golden strokes from head to toe, saw something in him worth saving. She encouraged him to join AA, which he did, and she also encouraged him to take his role as a father seriously for a change. Her love for us kids and her belief in the deeper part of him made him realize how long it had been since he'd done right by us, and it not only propelled him to get sober, it also motivated him to be a better man.

Our family's reaction to Shirley was a mixed one: my mother was jealous of her but happy my father had become more engaged as a parent; Gail hated her; my other sisters were indifferent; and I, despite my attachment to my mother, adored her. When she expressed wanting to marry my father, I was elated. I truly believed she was the best thing that could ever happen to him.

Shirley was an independent woman with her own financial reserves. She ran a private practice while also working for the school district, so she wasn't a wife who relied on her husband in the traditional way. She believed in equality and earned it without having to ask. I admired that about her and relished the attention she paid to me, prepping me for job interviews and supporting my passion for art. She even encouraged me to write and illustrate a children's book, believing I had something special to offer. I didn't pursue it at the time, but the mere fact that she thought so highly of me gave me the confidence that she would support me no matter the situation.

So while I had never outwardly claimed that Dan was my partner, or that I was anyone but a normal, heterosexual man, I was so unnerved and depressed by my circumstance with Dan that I decided to confide in Shirley.

I had made an appointment with her at her office, and she welcomed me with a giant hug as she always did. After motioning for me to sit opposite her, she said, "Now what's got you so down these days?"

Just hearing the caring in her voice felt like the permission I needed to break down. Erupting in tears, I confessed for the first time that Dan was my lover, my everything, and that our relationship had grown so dysfunctional and turbulent that I could no longer ride the emotional roller coaster I'd been on for the past three years.

When I looked up at her, she had a sympathetic smile on her face. She reached out and put her hand on my leg.

"Oh, Paul," she said. "That's a lot for one person to be dealing with."

I nodded as she handed me a tissue. "You must have helped a lot of people deal with tough relationships. What do you think I should do?"

Shirley thought for a moment, then spoke with calm assuredness. "Well, I think the first step is to deal with your sexuality."

I wiped my face. "What do you mean?"

"There's a treatment that's helping people like you. It's called aversion therapy."

My stomach tightened. I glanced away then back at her. "What's that?"

"It's where people who think they're gay undergo a kind of treatment to cure their unnatural thoughts. It has a lot of promise."

My heart fell. I loved Shirley, and I trusted her. And while she didn't condemn me for being gay, she clearly believed there was something wrong with it. A sickly feeling rushed through my body thinking of what the therapy would entail. But she was looking at me with such love, such sincere affection. I had struggled with my sexuality since I was a child, and I was miserable in my relationship. If she had a way to help me, perhaps I should do what she suggested.

"Okay," I agreed. "What do I need to do?"

For the next several weeks, I attended private aversion therapy sessions with a colleague of Shirley's. Each session consisted of being hooked up to electrodes and watching a series of images of heterosexual people in relationships, then flashing an intermittent image of a gay couple, which would administer a shock. The point was to "avert" me from so-called unnatural behavior with these shocks, so that out in the real world, I would no longer be drawn to it.

I was also encouraged to engage in physical acts with women. So, to her credit, Lynda became my guinea pig. But every time I kissed, touched, or attempted to have sex with her, the image of the mismatched floral jacket and plaid pants from that time on the beach flashed before me. Lynda and I would end up laughing, and I would report to the psychologist that I "did my homework," every bit of it a ruse.

Today, this kind of "therapy" is widely seen as appalling and sinister, as it should be, but in 1974, it was seen as a potential "cure" for a life-style most people had a hard time understanding. It was a rare person who embraced a gay man or woman with no question, no judgment, even in highly liberal Southern California. And no matter how natural it felt for me to be with men, the shame I had always felt fed into this theory of needing to be "fixed."

But after a few months of enduring the treatments, I felt worse than ever. My affinity for men was as strong as when I began, and it was clear that the therapy was unsuccessful for me. I told Shirley I wanted to stop, and though she conveyed sincere worry for me, she supported me in doing so, promising to honor our confidentiality and keep my sexuality a secret.

Dan, still swept up in his affairs, lies, and increased drug and alcohol use, had no idea what I had been going through.

CHAPTER SIXTEEN

1975

What a person believes is love can endure a lot, but not without consequences that can shape you for a lifetime.

In Dan's and my fourth year together, I lived with a completely unpredictable person. I never knew who I would come home to, who Dan would turn into at a club, who I was sharing my life with. I had a multitude of reasons to break up with him and move out, yet something in me, something I couldn't pinpoint, wouldn't let me leave. If I had made a pro/con list, it would have looked like this:

Pros	*Cons*
Our passion is still amazing	His drinking
He's taught me a lot	His drug use
I love our apartment	He lies constantly
He supports my school	He cheats on me
	I can't trust him
	He scares me sometimes
	He's erratic
	I've lost respect for him

But I was too immersed in our fire and ice to do anything as rational as make an actual pro and con list when it came to Dan. If I had, I imagine the words would have stared at me like an accusing authority. *Is this what you wanted?* I'd have heard. *Are the pros you wrote down good reasons to stay in a relationship? And those cons . . . isn't it obvious how dysfunctional this is?* Then the voice would perhaps soften like a compassionate friend. *This isn't you, Paul. This has never been the kind of relationship you dreamed of, not the way it is now. Don't you think you deserve better?*

At the thought of separating my life from Dan's, I closed my eyes and felt the tears burning behind my lids. Despite knowing it was the right thing to do, the idea of leaving him hurt worse than anything I could remember. More than the fifteen months in foster care. More than Misty dying. More than almost losing my hand. Even the worst of his offenses hadn't made me stop loving him. I had wondered why women stayed with abusive men—and now I understood it. That magic that draws you together, that spiritual tie, doesn't just die because one of you goes off the deep end. At least that's what I tried to convince myself, even as I stormed out of our apartment after yet another epic fight.

———

Over the next few weeks, I floated through my classes in a daze. My art projects all bore thick swashes of angry reds and despondent blacks, spattered with guilt and pain. When Dan and I spoke on the phone, it would end with me urging him to get help for his excessive drinking and drug use so that we could get back together, which would only tick him off. He would hang up on me, and I would collapse into myself, feeling irritatingly ill-equipped to be on my own without him.

But as much as I was angry at Dan for all the intolerable behavior that had caused our relationship to suffer, I didn't want my mother to know the ugly details. She and Dan loved each other deeply, and I wasn't going to upset her by trashing Dan in front of her. So I shoved my hurt feelings into a charcoal box behind my heart, hiding my depression from her the way I learned to do when I was five.

One night, during our short-lived first breakup, I decided to go hang out at the popular gay/piano bar in Laguna Beach called Little Shrimp. Dan and I had been there many times, but I had never been there without him. I was feeling a bit sentimental as I walked toward the door when a car drove by and I heard someone yell "faggot" out the window.

I turned around abruptly. "Why don't you come say that to my face!" I shouted.

The car screeched into a U-turn and headed back my way. Three guys tumbled out, one with a skateboard in his hand, and hastened toward me. Not one to back down when I was called derogatory names, I positioned myself for defense. All three guys approached me at once and lunged at me. For every punch I threw, I felt three blows to some part of my body. This went on for a couple minutes until, twisting and ducking, I managed to wrestle the skateboard out of the one guy's hand. I swung hard at one, knocking him in the skull, then repeated the move with another.

"I'll fucking kill you!" I screamed. "I'll fucking kill you!"

The two guys I took out with the skateboard were writhing on the ground. The other guy stumbled away from me, panting and wiping his mouth with the back of his hand. Then he turned around and pointed a pudgy finger at me. "This isn't over, you little fucker. We'll find your ass and kill you!"

I hurled the skateboard at them. "Go fuck yourselves!"

Hearing the commotion, a group of people ran out of the bar to find me beaten up pretty badly.

"Come on, man," someone said, shuffling me inside. "Let's get you cleaned up."

Fifteen minutes later, with the blood washed off my face and hands, revealing swollen mounds in multiple places, and Band-Aids only partially hiding a few open cuts, I looked like the guy who lost.

But to me, despite my distaste for violence, the only guys who lost were the ones who weren't willing to stand up for themselves in the face of bullies, whether their weapons were slurs, or fists, or both, to prove that someone's strength had nothing to do with his sexuality.

———

Inside a month, Dan and I were back together. The passionate makeup sex we always had was like bringing two strong, stubborn magnets together that had been separated; the natural pull was nearly impossible to break. Dan said he would try to cut back on his "recreational excess," and I wanted to be the supportive partner, so I let his word be an un-merited shade of gold, despite the nagging nudge inside that I might be giving him too much credit.

Within two weeks of moving back in, I found myself fretting for hours one night, waiting for Dan to come home. When he finally arrived after two a.m., he was high as a kite.

Dan was barely in the door when I greeted him with, "Is this what you call 'tapering off'?"

He looked at me like I had completely confounded him.

"Where've you been?" I said. "I've been so worried about you."

"Awww," he fake sniveled, "were you?"

"Dan, I'm serious. Look at you. How did you get home?"

He strode with a tilt into the room. "My lover drove me."

He laughed. I didn't.

"Oh, come on," he slurred, "I'm just joking."

"Fuck you. How do you think that makes me feel?"

He sidled over to me. "Oh babe, don't take it so seriously."

I could see him blacking out this scene, like so many drug- or booze-infused scenes in our relationship, not remembering a thing about it in the morning.

He tried to kiss me but I pushed him away. "Don't. Not when you're like this."

Dan made a "la-dee-dah" face. "Fine. I've had my fill tonight anyway."

I'm certain the hurt on my face was palpable, but Dan didn't seem to notice . . . or care.

Within a couple more weeks, Dan had completely returned to his old ways, and I realized that his promises were merely empty brown bags with my name written in bold, black marker.

I moved home once again feeling worse than ever.

———

Drowning in the pain of feeling abandoned by and unimportant to the man I loved most in the world, I started frequenting clubs and bars on the nights I wasn't working at the hotel, occasionally picking up guys who showed me the slightest interest. Though I felt like those prostitutes on the street I felt sorry for, and the sex was as dissatisfying physically and emotionally as ever, I was desperate to feel some semblance of being loved. Drugs and alcohol, though I did use them to an extent, were never a way I used to fill myself up, so fleeting infatuation and shameful sex were my abusive substances of choice. It made no sense, and deep down I knew it, but I chose to ignore the cracking of my soul in favor of feeling like I mattered to someone, however briefly or shallow.

One night at one of the clubs, I met a good-looking guy who invited me over to his place. Even though something about him unsettled me, I agreed to drive him home since he had come with a friend. When we arrived at his apartment, it was in one of the sleaziest neighborhoods I'd ever seen—and I'd practically grown up in the projects, so that was saying a lot. Gauzy drapes were billowing out the windows, and it sat above a liquor store. Had I followed him there, I would have taken off at the first sight of the place. But because he was in my car, I felt like I didn't have much choice but to go in for a bit. He walked me up a couple flights of stairs, then opened the door with a sly smile.

At least a hundred candles were burning on every surface. "Shit," I said.

"What?"

"Isn't it dangerous to leave all these candles burning for hours?"

"Nah," he said, waltzing inside and peeling off his leather jacket. "Besides, it's all for you."

We had only just met, so clearly it was for *someone*, but not necessarily *me*. I glanced around, completely creeped out by the scene, feeling like I had just entered the den of a cult. When I turned around, the guy was already leaning over a small mirror, dividing lines of coke with a blade.

"Come on," the guy said. I had conceded to do coke on occasion with Dan, although I hated the way he never knew when to quit the way I did. So, figuring I'd play this guy's game for a short time and then go, I walked over to him as he snorted a line, stood up for a few seconds, then bent down and snorted another. I followed by taking a line myself.

We played around a bit. He peeled off my shirt and I kicked off my shoes. Though the last thing I wanted was to let him touch me, I was driven by my ridiculous mindset that I was getting back at Dan. We finished off the lines he had and knocked back a couple small drinks. Always mindful of being in control, I had let him have a lot more coke than I did.

Suddenly, the guy jumped up. He dashed into the kitchen and started rummaging through drawers.

"Shit! That can't be all I had!" He launched into a panic and darted into the bedroom, then darted back looking crazed. "Fuck!"

His pulsating anxiety set off an alarm in me. In a flash, I pictured him snapping and me becoming the victim at a possibly unintended but horrible crime scene. I could sense that he wouldn't willingly let me leave, so I hatched a quick lie.

"That's okay," I said, reaching for my shirt. "I have some coke in my car."

"No!" he said, clearly paranoid. "You can't put your shirt or shoes back on. Just go get it the way you are. And make it fast."

I knew better than to arouse suspicion by insisting, so I placated him while I retrieved my keys from my jacket.

"I'll be right back," I assured him.

Within seconds, I was running barefoot down the stairs toward my car. I hastily unlocked the door as I heard his shoes thudding on the metal steps after me. I plopped into the driver's seat, which was next to the curb, and sparked the ignition. Just as I was about to shut the door, he appeared next to me in a rage.

"You bastard! You can't leave!"

He reached out to grab me. I threw the car into reverse, smacking him hard with the open door and sending him flying. Then I threw the car into drive and skidded off. Glancing into the rearview mirror, I saw him jump up, then watched his flailing silhouette and ringing expletives slowly become one with the darkness.

Slightly impaired from the drugs and booze, but acutely alert from the adrenaline rush, I drove home with the realization that I was not only falling deeper down a well of shame, but that it was likely I had just escaped serious injury or death yet another time in my life.

I was also pissed that I had to leave a favorite shirt, jacket, and pair of shoes behind.

————

Dan and I got back together two more times over the next several months, both of which ended in harsh accusations, a vulgar shouting match, and me moving into my mom's apartment yet again for a handful of days or weeks. His continued addiction to abusive substances and my addiction to him were a recipe for disaster, yet it didn't stop me from making every effort to stabilize and balance our relationship.

Though I knew he perceived it as nagging, I continued to encourage Dan to pull back from his toxic overindulgences. He would make me tentative promises to curtail them, which for a time was enough for me, and our passion never waned, so I put up with more than I ever should have because when times were good, I had never felt so loved in my life. I had the sense to know it was unhealthy, damaging even, but I still tried to convince myself that things would change between Dan and me, even as we drifted further apart.

The truth was that at twenty-two, with those broad, violet strokes of magnetic attraction obscuring all rationale, I couldn't see the deeper reasons I had tied my soul to a man who in many ways, wasn't so unlike my father.

One night, after Dan came stumbling home well past midnight after another drinking and drug binge with his friends after work, I'd had it.

"Where the hell have you been?" I shouted. "Doing more drugs with your so-called 'employees' until you can't see straight?"

He turned around and squinted at me. "Oh, don't start with that shit! I'm not the only one who has fun. You do it too."

"But I'm always in control, Dan. I know when to stop. You don't!"

Dan threw his keys across the room and they hit the bookcase with a clang. "I'm so sick of you telling me how in control you are, like I'm the one who has a problem!"

"You ARE the one who has a problem!"

"That's your opinion," he said. He walked toward me like he wanted to punch me. "Why can't you just let me be me?" he yelled. "Why are you always trying to change me?"

"Because look at you! You're a fucking mess!"

"Well, if that's what you think, why don't you take your self-righteous ass and get the fuck out once and for all!"

I might have had my flaws, and I might have stooped to his level in ways I wasn't proud of, but there was one thing I wasn't, and that was self-righteous.

"How dare you call me self-righteous! What a fucking hypocrite!"

"Whatever, Paul, you little prick!" He was breathing heavy and his eyes burned with disdain. "I'm serious. If that's what you think of me, then get the fuck OUT!"

My heart pummeled my chest like a jackhammer demolishing a once handsome street that had fallen into disrepair. In that moment, as in so many other nasty moments between us, I wanted to lunge at him and let my fists fly. Like the night those assholes called me a faggot, I had never been one to let anyone mistreat me without a fight, not even Dan. And I knew instinctively that this could get ugly if I let it.

"Fine," I yelled. "That's exactly what I'm going to do. I am so DONE with this shit!"

Dan just smirked as I left the room and threw my things together. When I returned to the living room with my bags slung over my shoulder, Dan was on the couch smoking a cigarette, as if our relationship didn't just end for good, as if I was heading out at 3:00 a.m. for a joyride.

I stood across from him until he looked at me.

"This is it, Dan. Don't think I'm ever coming back to put up with any more of your bullshit."

"Good," Dan said nonchalantly. "Go."

With that I took a last quick glance around the apartment that had been my home for the last five years, some of them the best of my life, some the worst. Then I turned and walked out the door, slamming it behind me for the last time.

The next day, I woke up on the couch in the two-bedroom apartment my mother shared with my two younger sisters. To say that I felt like a child whose big boy ideas hadn't worked out after all is an understatement. The truth was that the hurt I felt seemed so insurmountable that I wanted to die.

CHAPTER SEVENTEEN

In the midst of Dan's and my dramatic breakups and reunions, I had somehow managed to graduate from college. After starting out in school as the kid who couldn't concentrate, the kid who wasn't good at the basics, the kid who had to repeat kindergarten, I had fulfilled the dream my mother always had for me—and believed I would accomplish. Now it was time to truly be on my own as an adult and choose a career path, but I was still reeling from Dan's and my breakup. What's more, my art major didn't automatically open big doors.

In spite of—or perhaps because of—my humble beginnings as a student, I was drawn to teaching. So I enrolled in a student teaching program during the day and continued working at the hotel at night. I had stashed enough money away from my licentious encounters with well-paying guests to give those propositions up completely. Not only was I disgusted with myself for doing it, I didn't want anything to jeopardize my path as a teacher. Being perceived as gay in the educational system at that time was enough of a challenge to hide—not to mention the dysfunctional pull I still felt toward Dan, and that he made known, through frequent phone calls, he still felt toward me. Veering back into his lane, I knew, was an option that could only end in a crash, but it tugged at me constantly nonetheless.

Though I had gotten my own apartment after moving out of Dan's, my mother thought that moving home for a while would help me save money. I reluctantly agreed, but there was one thing I wanted to buy first: an ultra cool car.

When I arrived at the lot and saw the shiny copper Datsun 240Z with velvet seats, I was sold. In its own distorted way, it filled the demolition zone inside my heart where the remaining embers of Dan's and my relationship still sparked and smoldered with a poisonous mix of hope and futility. Driving that car to school and work, and escorting my mom in it on shopping and lunch or dinner dates, made me feel as if those days of visualizing my ideal life were beginning to materialize. A huge piece of that ideal life was missing, and I hadn't arrived at complete independence yet, but it was definitely a step in a new and promising direction.

As a student teacher, I was assigned to all different types of classrooms—from high income to low income—and I loved the experience in all of them. For whatever reason, teaching came easily to me. I knew instinctively that the way to connect with children wasn't to instill fear or impose harsh rules, the way Mrs. Secker and other teachers of mine had, but to encourage their curiosity and bring out their natural gifts in a structured but playful way. It also helped that I related to the kids no matter their background, especially to the ones who were struggling.

The days I spent in the various schools were akin to the high I felt when I was creating art. In its own way, that's what teaching is: developing some level of raw material in a child into something tangible—an understanding or passion or confidence that wasn't necessarily there before. When a light would go on behind a child's eyes, or when he conquered a task that had been difficult, I felt a gratification like no other. Being part of the kids' evolution was not only a humbling position to be in, it also lent a level of healing to my own wounded soul.

Over the months, I was lauded for my off-the-cuff ideas that engaged the kids, and for my ability to work with all ages and personalities. The feeling of accomplishment I felt was greater than any I'd ever experienced; it also took some of the pain away and filled the void of Dan's and my breakup. But perhaps best of all was that my mother was over-the-moon proud of me.

One day, I came home on a high from my day with the kids, excited to share it with my mom, to find her on the couch, her eyes a million miles from our living room. I sat down next to her.

"Hey," I said, touching her arm, "is something wrong?"

She took a long deep breath and turned to face me. "I have a lump in my breast."

My heart skipped and I felt my stomach twist into a tormented skein. "You do? How big is it?"

She sighed. "About the size of a silver dollar."

I glanced away. Everyone in my mother's family had died of one type of cancer or another, so we both knew this was nothing to take lightly. I met her eyes again. "How long has it been there?"

"About two months."

I grasped her hand, instantly inflating with worry. "Well, I don't think we should wait any longer to get you looked at."

She nodded. "I guess not."

The next week, my sisters and I took my mother in for tests. When the biopsy came back malignant, all four of us siblings were terrified.

"I recommend that your mother have a mastectomy immediately," the doctor told us. "Then we need to follow that with radiation and chemotherapy."

We looked at each other, all of us tormented by the thought of our mother going through such a radical surgery and treatment. I wondered, too, about the additional care she would need. Gail was already married with two little girls; Noel was still in high school; and I was consumed with working days as a student teacher and nights at the hotel, not to mention that I had never been one to deal well with illness or to excel at caregiving.

Seeming to read my mind, Tina volunteered, "I'll take a leave of absence from school and take care of Mom."

Tina had opted to live at home while going to college, but it was still a big sacrifice for her to make, especially with the added responsibility she'd be taking on.

"Are you sure?" Gail asked.

Tina nodded. "I'm sure."

"Because it might be a lot for you," Gail added.

Tina nodded assuredly. "I can handle it. I don't want you guys worrying about it."

"We'll help you," Noel offered.

"I know you will," Tina said with a smile.

When we shared the news with our mother, she merely nodded as if she wasn't surprised by the test results or the doctor's recommendations. She wasn't in favor of Tina leaving school to care for her, but conceded when we all convinced her it would only be temporary. Displaying a bold front, my mother nodded resolutely with a brave smile. But when I wrapped my arms around her, I could feel her body clench with the release of her tears, falling in tandem with mine.

After my mother went through with the mastectomy, Tina, true to her word, spent day and night providing for my mother's every need. Whatever resided within her that felt driven to be our mother's nurturer, Tina was every bit the dedicated daughter. She drove my mom to all her appointments and treatments, and never once did she complain or ask for anything from us siblings. Slowly, my mother got better, and we all had hope that she would make a full recovery.

———

Six months after my mother's surgery, I graduated with my K–College multiple-subjects teaching credential, and my mother insisted on throwing me a party to celebrate. She was feeling a bit stronger by that point, and I could see from the sparkle in her eyes that had been dormant for a while how much it meant to her to do it. So, I agreed to the party as long as she allowed me to help.

"Fine," she said, "but I want there to be a few surprises."

Knowing how in love I was with the beach, my mother rented a cottage up on a hill in Laguna—a ritzy Southern California beach town about fifteen miles south of her apartment—that overlooked downtown. She invited the whole family, and I asked some of my closest friends to come.

When the evening of the festivities arrived, my mother and I were making the food when she discovered we were missing a few things. The grocery store was only a short walk away, and she insisted on running out while I stayed with everyone. But after a half hour went by and she hadn't returned, I began to get worried.

"Oh, she probably started chatting with the checker," someone said. "You know how everyone loves your mom. I'm sure she's fine."

But something inside told me she wasn't fine.

Soon after, we heard sirens. I looked out from our vantage point on the hill and saw flashing red lights in the distance. But since they weren't on the street where the store was, I figured it was a false alarm.

About twenty minutes later, there was a knock on the door. I opened it to find an officer on the porch. "Are you related to Ramona Ecke?" he asked.

"Yes," I said, swallowing hard as my family gathered around me in the doorway. "I'm her son."

He cleared his throat. "I'm sorry to have to tell you this, but your mother's in the hospital. She was in a fairly serious accident, but she's going to be okay."

"Oh my God," I whispered. "Was she hit by a car?"

"No," the cop said. "The car rolled and she flew out of it. But like I said, she'll be okay."

The car rolled and she flew out of it? What car?

I wanted to ask more questions, but instead I said, "We'll be right there."

My sisters and I moved like bumper cars trying not to crash into each other as they grabbed their purses and I scooped up my keys.

"You guys are welcome to stay," I said to the group, "but I don't know when we'll be back."

"Just go," someone said. "Don't worry about us."

My sisters piled into Gail's car and I followed them like a man possessed, desperate to see my mother and understand how she could have flown out of a car. When we arrived at the hospital, her entire head was bandaged and she had scrapes on her face that were covered with gauze. Her arm was heavily bandaged as well. Conscious but groggy from the heavy dose of pain medication and woozy from a concussion, she offered as much spunk as she could muster when she saw us. "Oh," she said. "I didn't mean for you to leave the party."

"Are you serious?" Tina said. "There's nowhere else we'd be than here with you."

"I appreciate that. But I'll be all right," she assured us.

It was distressing to see her so banged up, especially after everything she'd been through in the last months. Fussing with the fluid bag, the nurse pointed with her head. "That's a third-degree burn on her arm. It'll require at least one graft. But overall, she's pretty lucky."

"Now . . ." my mother said, "don't go worrying my kids."

The nurse gave a knowing nod and tossed a wry smile our way, then she checked the readings on the machines once more and left us alone with her.

"Mom," I said, "We don't understand. They said you were in a car accident. How could that be?"

She looked away for a moment, then blinked a few times and breathed in. "Well, I was tired after I walked to the store."

"Okay . . . but that doesn't explain . . ." I looked at my sisters then back at her. "They said you flew out of a car, like a convertible."

My mother glanced away again.

"Mom. What's going on?" I said gently. "There's something you're not telling us."

She hesitated. "Well, when I was in line at the store, I started chatting with the nice man behind me. He was very handsome and he thought I was pretty. I told him about your graduation party, and he thought it sounded wonderful."

She was struggling for coherence, so we cut her some slack for putting the missing puzzle pieces together in small bites.

"And . . . ?" Gail said.

"And . . . after I paid, the man offered to help carry my bags to the car. When I told him I'd walked, he said he could drive me back in his Ferrari. Well, I couldn't say no to that, could I?"

We all exchanged concerned glances but said nothing. I could imagine how this man's flattering words, and his paying attention to her in what probably seemed a genuine way, made my mother light up inside and feel attractive for the first time in years.

"So," she continued, "I got into his red convertible . . . it was so nice, honey," she said to me. "You would have loved it. But instead of driving me straight back, he asked if I'd like to see the view from the top of the hill. So I said okay, as long as it doesn't take too long. But he started driving way too fast up the winding road and he lost control around a curve. We went up on two wheels and then the car flipped over and went down the hill. That's when I flew out."

She was so matter-of-fact about it, it was odd. Perhaps it was the meds, but she was more animated relaying that one of her friends went to a bad hairdresser and was unhappy with the result.

"Mom!" Noel said. "You could have died!"

"But I didn't."

"No, but you could have."

"But I didn't. And because I didn't, we need to get back to your party. I can't let that get ruined."

"Mom," I said, taking her hand. "That's crazy. You can't just leave. You have a third-degree burn that needs surgery, you have a concussion . . . my party is *not* that important."

She looked me square in the eye. "It's that important to *me*. This is your celebration for working so hard. I'm not dead, so I'm going to be there."

Thirty minutes later, my mother somehow cajoled the doctor into releasing her with more pain medication and a promise to return the next day for a follow-up and to arrange for the first graft.

He made it clear it was against his better judgment. "Only if she rides in an ambulance," he insisted. She agreed, and fifteen minutes later, paramedics had her settled in for the ride.

We all returned to the party, but what had begun as a celebration of my milestone accomplishment rightly shifted to an unspoken celebration that my mother had survived yet another tragic turn in her life.

CHAPTER EIGHTEEN

After my mother recovered from several skin grafts, and her cancer went dormant for a time, she got her first job, working at Knott's Berry Farm—a famous local amusement park—in the historic school-house. The position required little exertion—she merely had to dress in period clothing and represent the Old West schoolteacher as guests filed through on a guided tour, but she enjoyed it immensely.

In a sweet twist of synchronicity, the school district offered me a teaching position—not in my own classroom, but an opportunity to work with the gifted children in various schools. I was flattered; it was a position not typically offered to someone with a fresh credential, and I eagerly accepted it.

Each week, I traveled to five different campuses, taking the children labeled "gifted" out of their main classrooms and into my assigned bungalow for a few hours. With the freedom to create curriculum I deemed appropriate for the different age groups, my creativity took flight like a hundred balloons, each its own shade of magic.

When selected teachers would pop in to observe me, I would consistently hear comments like, "I would have never thought of doing that!" or "What a fun idea!" or "Look how the kids are loving this!" At times, I almost felt like the Thomas Edison of the classroom. Bold new ideas came to me regularly, and when I executed them, they were nearly always a hit. It didn't take long before the administration started sitting in and taking notes. Within six months, my superior called me into his office for a meeting.

"Paul, as you know, we've been observing your work with the students. And I have to say, for a new teacher, you have a great deal of talent."

I beamed. "Thank you."

"And you seem to love interacting with the kids."

"I do," I said sincerely. "The kids are great."

He drew in a breath. "So we've been discussing it, the administration and I, and we'd like to offer you a bit more visible role."

I raised my eyebrows. I had only expected a review, not any kind of promotion. "Really?"

"Yes. With your innovative ideas and how well you relate to the children, we all agree that you would make an excellent head of the GATE program."

My mouth dropped open slightly. GATE stood for Gifted and Talented Education, and only certain schools in the district were able to host the celebrated program. It was implemented to give advanced students more creative and interactive curriculum, which was an incredible opportunity for a teacher to truly bring the classroom alive.

He continued. "You would oversee the GATE classes in each of the schools in the district, meet with the teachers, collaborate on projects, work with their students, that kind of thing. You'd basically make your own schedule . . . check in here in the morning and leave your plans for the day, then make your rounds. Does that sound like something you'd like to do?"

I was stunned. This kind of offer was unheard of for a twenty-three-year-old male, especially one who had barely had a chance to make an impact. The fact that they saw me as capable of holding such a prestigious position in this early stage of my career was a considerable boost to my self-esteem.

"It definitely does," I said. "I'm very flattered."

"And you'll receive a higher salary, of course. A fifteen percent raise."

I nodded. "Great."

He fanned out his hands. "So you're in?"

Always one for a new adventure, I mirrored his gesture. "I'm in."

We shook hands and I walked out on a high, blown away that I—at my young age—would be influencing new and seasoned teachers alike with my ideas. *My* ideas. And I didn't even have to spend years aspiring for the job or wrangle a hard-won interview. They came to *me*.

I used to wonder if I was somehow damned for being who I was, I thought, *but how could that be true when I've been given a gift like this?*

I was immersed in hatching project plans that summer, eager for the new school year to begin in the fall, when we found out that my mother's cancer had returned. It had traveled to her other breast, making it swell and start to turn black. Having heard of an alternative medicine clinic just across the border that used Laetrile, an extract of apricot kernels that had promising results, along with other natural healing modalities, we as a family arranged for her to receive treatment there. It was late in the game according to her oncologist, but we refused to give up on our mother without a fight.

The treatment, we learned, would require at least a three-week stay in Tijuana. So, without missing a beat, Tina said she would accompany her on the trip.

The Laetrile helped to improve my mother's health enough to buy her some more time, but despite our best efforts, we were told there was nothing more they could do.

So Tina continued to be her nurturer at home, and I finally realized that the time I had with my mother was more finite than I'd grasped before. I might not have been a natural caregiver, but I did know how much she had missed feeling beautiful, so I made it my mission to give that feeling back to her in every way I could.

She had always been embarrassed that she couldn't afford to fix the broken front tooth she'd had for years, so I dipped into my stash and got her fitted with a shiny new cap. She had also lost a lot of her excess weight, so I took her on shopping trips for clothes that flattered her slimmer figure, instead of the muumuus and oversized blouses she had been hiding in for years. I relished watching her turn her head left, then right, then left again in the hairdresser's mirror, lightly touching her updated hairstyle with a sparkle in her eye. We had long talks over fancy meals at restaurants, and I even decorated her apartment with some new art and accessories that made her new smile even brighter.

But despite all the bonding we did as we faced her mortality, and in spite of the fact that she had always embraced my relationship with Dan, never pushing me to admit that it was more than friends, though she certainly knew it was, I could never bring myself to tell my mother I was gay. Even in her last days, when she asked me point blank with her sweet way, one that carried no judgment or worry, something inside me held fast to the guise. Perhaps knowing in my heart that she knew, but simply never prodded me for confirmation, absolved me from the admission. With every sign that she would—and already had—accept that the boy she created was perfect just as he was, I still adamantly denied it.

I had no idea that I wasn't the only one who had spent the better part of his life fiercely protecting a secret he believed would shatter the lives of those around him forever.

CHAPTER NINETEEN

1978

Though I had cultivated a futile habit of hoping something would change despite all the signs that it wouldn't, I still maintained hope that my mother, my sweet, beautiful, loving but wounded mother, would somehow beat the cancer, the cancer I would have gladly taken so that she could live. The cancer that paid no attention to the fact that she was only forty-nine and still had plenty of life in front of her. The cancer that manifested from all the anxiety and stress she felt from the nurturing she couldn't always provide her children.

But on the twenty-first of October, at home with all her children and with the aid of hospice, the cancer finally won its three-year crusade against my mother's body.

Dan, who had been her second son, showed up at the funeral as devastated as I was. Having no one else to turn to who understood the pain I was feeling, I fell into Dan's arms and into the comfort of his empathy.

Holding me the way I had missed, he whispered, "Maybe we should get back together." The longing, aching part of me was tempted, but everything about it was wrong—the timing, the history between us, his still wild lifestyle.

"No," I said after a pause that lasted too long, gently pulling away. "I think that would be a mistake."

His bright blue eyes conveyed that he knew I was probably right.

"But I want to be there for you," he assured me.

"Thank you," I said. "I know you're missing her too."

He nodded as tears filled his eyes. "I am."

He held me again as we both let our emotions escape into each other's circle of sensitivity—and I won a notch in my maturity for not caving into reconciliation when I was at my most vulnerable.

A few days later, I was at my mom's apartment, tackling the nearly un-bearable task of going through her things with my sisters. While the girls were sorting out her clothes, I picked up the handbag I had bought her that she loved so much. Inside, I found her wallet. I slowly ran my fingers over the well-worn leather, imagining how many times her hands had held it, then opened it to find photos of us kids in their prominent plastic holder. I gingerly flipped through them all, most of them from when we were small. She didn't have any credit cards or much cash, but she did have handfuls of business cards poking out of the other compartments. I was fanning through them, keeping certain ones and tossing others, when I came across a picture of a baby boy. Not recognizing him, I turned the photo over. The words "My Loving Son" were scrolled on the back. My heart skipped a beat. I flipped the picture back over and looked at it more closely. There was a familiarity about the boy, but he definitely wasn't me. Then I found another photo of the same boy, at maybe two years old. Again, the back was inscribed with "My Loving Son." Behind those were a few pictures of Laura, the name they gave our sister who had been given up for adoption. I had seen those photos before, but the two snapshots of the little boy perplexed me.

"Hey, Gail," I said. "Look at this."

"What is it?" she asked, coming over.

"Have you ever seen this baby?"

She took the photos and stared at them for a few seconds. "No. Who is he?"

"Look on the back."

Gail's mouth dropped open as she read the handwriting. She looked up at me and whispered, "You don't think . . .?"

"I don't know what to think."

"But he can't be . . . can he? Mom wouldn't lie about something that huge."

Neither of us wanted to believe that our mother would carry a secret of that magnitude. But all my life, I had longed for a brother. When I was finally going to have one, though we knew he wasn't my father's child, my mother came home and told us he had died. Or had he?

I shrugged. "I don't know. But I want to find out."

In the months that followed, I gave my best effort to focus on my new position as head of the GATE program, swallowing my grief in the classroom and eclipsing it with unbridled enthusiasm. But I could only keep up the ruse for so long before I craved a break.

In my mother's last weeks, I had suffered constant worry about her health. In my attempt to cope with the stress, I would sign in and go to my first school of the day, then make a pitstop at my apartment, where I could collapse on the couch and find numbing solace in glass after glass of wine, as Donna Summer's *On the Radio* album spun repeatedly on the turntable like an anthem of comfort.

Macarthur Park . . . is melting . . . in the dark . . .

Someone found the letter you wrote me on the radio . . .

Dim all the lights, sweet darling, 'cause tonight it's all the way . . .

I would promise myself a half hour, but the half hours turned into hours, and I would never make it to my second school. Though I was a fairly free agent as my schedule went, I feared the district would get wind of my afternoon detours—but I was so distraught over my mother's illness that I simply didn't care.

Now that my mother was gone, the routine continued to wrap me in a dysfunctional blanket of condolence. But on Halloween night, ten days after she passed, I decided to try to lift the veil from my funk by hanging out at Little Shrimp, the popular piano bar in Laguna Beach I loved.

I strolled in to the pianist banging out a perfect rendition of "I Feel the Earth Move" as the crowd, under a buffalo snow–like layer of smoke, echoed the lyrics. I was one of the few people there not in costume, so I just ordered a beer and hung out near the bar for a bit. Some friends waved hello from across the room, but I really wasn't much in the mood for being social, and it was pretty crowded, so I waved back then eased out.

Once outside, I decided to mosey a block down the street to another iconic gay bar called The Boom Boom Room. With its illustrious history—Rock Hudson and Paul Lynde were known to party there, along with celebrities like Bette Davis and Bette Midler—and its celebrated drag queen nights, it was a mecca for the gay community. Teeming with people in outlandish costumes, it was even more crowded than Little Shrimp. But I managed to squeeze myself next to a pole and lean against it, with just enough room to faintly groove to the beat of Blondie's "Heart of Glass."

Once I had a love and it was divine
Soon found out I was losing my mind . . .

I rolled my eyes and nodded knowingly to myself. *Don't I know it.*

As Blondie's voice faded and the jukebox clicked into Gloria Gaynor's, a guy edged his way next to me.

"Hi," he said, raising his voice over the song. "I'm Bill."

I looked his way and was immediately drawn into his piercing blue eyes, not so unlike Dan's.

In spite of the grief I was cloaked in, I smiled. "I'm Paul."

"Can I buy you a drink?" he asked.

"Sure. A vodka tonic?"

He nodded and disappeared. When he returned several minutes later, "Love Is Like Oxygen" was pulsing through the melange of cologne and cigarettes that wove throughout the room. The lyrics weren't lost on me.

"Here you go," he said, handing me the drink.

"Thanks."

He glanced around then back at me. "Some costumes, huh?"

"Yeah." I took a sip. "Why aren't you dressed up?"

He shrugged. "It's not really my thing. You?"

"Just wasn't in the mood, I guess."

He nodded. "Well, that's good. I might not have sought you out if you'd been in disguise."

I half-laughed.

"Actually," he confessed, "I saw you at Little Shrimp and wanted to meet you, but then I saw you leave. So I followed you here."

Mesmerized by his cerulean eyes, and flattered by his interest, I said, "You did?"

He laughed. "Don't worry. I'm not a stalker. I just thought you were cute."

I laughed too, then I looked him up and down. "You're not bad yourself."

Feeling comfortable with him right away, my grief graciously stepped behind the scenes, as if an angel had nudged it, and we fell into easy conversation. It turned out that we were both teachers. He had four sisters and I had three, and we discovered that we'd both grown up with alcoholic parents. Our similarities carried a level of comfort, but underlying that was the intense attraction I felt to him, and that all signs pointed to him feeling toward me. It wasn't long before we leaned in and kissed each other. Electricity shot through my body as A Taste of Honey's "Boogie Oogie Oogie" morphed into the gentle sway of the Bee Gees' "How Deep Is Your Love."

We pulled apart slowly. "Want to go to my place?" Bill asked.

I smiled. "Let's go."

For the next three days, Bill and I barely left his bed. Feeling mildly guilty, we called in sick to our districts, spending each day and night talking, caressing each other, and making love.

Lying face to face, with Bill stroking my shoulder, I couldn't help but see a possible future with him. Bill's Scandinavian good looks and tall, fit physique were exactly what I was attracted to physically; he was drawn to darker men, so he found my German/Italian ancestry, naturally tan complexion, and muscular build alluring. What's more, we shared a level of connection akin to that I had only ever shared with Dan. Yet with Bill, no toxic addiction hovered between us. In the brief time I had spent with him, he had already demonstrated the caring and sensitivity of a true gentleman, the kind of man I had always dreamed of one day spending my life with.

As I fell asleep in his arms, it was as if I felt a wink from my mother, a sign that I was finally somehow home.

———

For the next six months, Bill and I saw each other regularly. He was a huge comfort to me over the loss of my mother, and he was not only sensitive and caring, he was also grounded and nurturing, which was exactly what I needed in a partner.

Several nights a week, Bill would drive the thirty miles from his beach cottage in Dana Point to my apartment in Orange, and we would meet at our favorite bars and clubs in Laguna Beach on weekends.

At the time, I had three roommates, one of whom was Lynda. Being my sister/friend/confidante all rolled into one for years, she would frequently climb into my bed at night just to talk. The first night Bill stayed over, Lynda crept into my room and, surprised to find a man in my bed, stood quietly staring over him, as if sizing him up for approval. When Bill sensed her presence, he woke with a start.

Lynda gasped. "Wow," she exclaimed, "you have the most beautiful blue eyes!"

Instead of being startled, or even creeped out by a lurking woman over my bed, Bill broke into a huge grin, and they were great friends from that moment on.

With Lynda's overwhelming endorsement of Bill and me as a couple, and our growing closeness, we decided we wanted to make our relationship an exclusive one. Though Dan and I had never gotten back together, I was still caving to trysts with him on occasion, and Bill was dating someone else off and on, but we agreed that we would each cut those ties in favor of complete monogamy. Dan didn't understand my desire to stop our rendezvous, and I would have struggled with it too—had something significant not changed.

Ever since being placed in foster care, I have suffered with severe abandonment issues. The mere idea of anyone leaving me—from something as big as a relationship to as seemingly insignificant as a friend departing a club before I do—sends me into feelings of panic and even short-lived depression. The thought of Dan leaving me had always been too much for me to bear; it was my mother leaving me—first at the Fletchers' home for an indefinite period, then every time she came and went on her weekend visits—all over again. But my decision to leave *him*, and my assertion to cut off our sporadic affair, was different. Yes, it still hurt, but I was the one in control of the situation, and therefore not the child left behind, shuddering in that cold, toxic stew of wondering, *What did I do wrong? What did I do to deserve this?*

Plus, I wasn't leaving this time out of anger or spite. I had held on to Dan's and my connection because he was my touchstone, but now I had Bill. Securely under his protective wing, I felt free to move from the perceived rock that was Dan to the tangible rock that was Bill. In many ways, it was like being picked up by my angel mother and handed to my soul mate.

Only time would tell if a stable future together wasn't merely another fantasy beanstalk I believed I could climb, a fairy tale yearning to be realized in the mind of a lifelong boy dreamer.

CHAPTER TWENTY

1979

The first year Bill and I were together, I walked a tightrope of mixed emotions. The balancing pole would dip right, pulled by my intense grief over my mother's death, then left with the lepidopteran flutters of being in love with someone new. In the middle, where there should have been some balance and calm, I was grappling with something that confused me immensely: my inability to feel completely comfortable and fulfilled sexually.

Dan's and my passion had been so consuming that I never once questioned that part of our relationship. But he was also my first love— and first sexual experience. Every time I had strayed to get back at him, or accepted money for a hotel guest's quick fix, I never felt any satisfaction in the encounters. I figured it was because I wasn't in love with any of those men, and I was simply old-fashioned that way—for sex to have meaning, I had to be in love.

But now I *was* in love again, and Bill was a wonderful lover, so I knew my unease had nothing to do with him. Yet something inside me was afraid to feel. Was it the idea that my mother's being gone meant that she could somehow "see" me with Bill? That the shame I had carried and the secret I'd always kept from her was now something she knew for a fact?

I didn't have a good answer.

I only had a growing pain inside that if I was deficient in this arena, something might be wrong with me after all.

———

Navigating my duality like the champ that I was at it, I continued in my position as head of the GATE program, ensconced in a glowing heterosexual façade, while on weekends I partied with Bill at gay bars, the only place I could be my authentic self in public.

In playing this constant game of "conceal and pretend," along with hopping from side to side of my emotional teeter totter, I had little energy and zero time to pursue any type of art, which my mother had encouraged me to never abandon.

I had also had to stuff my burning curiosity about the identity of that mysterious little boy I'd found covertly tucked away in my mother's wallet.

One day, Lynda and I met out for drinks after work. After catching up with small talk, I decided to tell her about the photos I'd found after the funeral.

She glanced away and her expression shifted uncomfortably.

"Lynda?" I said, growing serious, knowing she had never been one to keep anything from me. "What's with the face?"

She took a deep breath. "I know who that boy is."

My heart sped up. "You do? Who is he?"

She looked away again, seeming to contemplate her role in the secret. "I'm not supposed to know."

"Okay," I acknowledged impatiently. "But you *do*. So tell me."

She bit the inside of her mouth. "Okay, but I don't know how you're going to feel about it."

My eyes widened.

"Paul," she said, putting her hand over mine. "That boy is your brother."

My heart leapt and dropped at the same time. "How?" I said. "My mom said he died."

She nodded. "I know."

"But why? Was something wrong with him?"

Lynda's mouth curved with tenderness. "No, nothing was wrong with him . . . except that he wasn't your dad's." She rolled her eyes and I mirrored her. "So your mom came to my mom and asked for help to find an adoptive family for him."

"But why couldn't she just keep him? We all would have helped her take care of him."

Lynda knew I wanted a brother more than anything growing up, but she also had sympathy for my mother. "Because your mom didn't want that pressure on you. And she'd been through so much already . . ."

My eyes welled thinking of those tumultuous years she endured with my father. "So what did your mom do?"

"She knew a couple who was looking to adopt. So she told them about the baby, and she was involved somehow—I don't know how exactly—with coordinating the adoption. Your mom never met the couple, I don't think. It was all very hush hush. I wasn't even supposed to know."

A tear fell down my cheek. "So my mom just gave my brother away?"

Lynda squeezed my hand. "I'm sorry, sweetie. I know it's *really* hard for you to find out like this." She paused, seeming to search for a comforting explanation. "I think after what you guys went through after your parents gave up Laura, your mom thought it would be cruel to make you go through it again. I think she probably thought that if you believed the baby had died, you'd have some closure or something."

I thought about it for a moment. A small part of me imagined how hard it must have been for my mother to give up another child. But a bigger part of me was angry and hurt.

"So I had to miss out on knowing I had a brother because she thought it was best?"

Lynda squeezed my hand again. "Would it have been easier knowing he'd been adopted?"

I wiped my face. "I don't know. Maybe. Maybe not. I don't know." I wiped my face again. "All I know is, I want to find him now that I know he's alive."

Lynda nodded in understanding. "Okay. I'll talk to my mom and see what I can find out."

———

The next day, Lynda called, but the news wasn't what I wanted to hear.

The baby's adoption was not only closed, his parents were extremely sensitive about it. Despite the fact that the mother was Asian and the baby clearly wasn't her biological child, she fiercely protected her mother role, threatened by the idea of her son having anything to do with his birth family. Edna, Lynda's mother, was friends with the couple, and when she had visited after the adoption, she had snapped a photo here and there on the sly and slipped them to my mother. As my mother was denied any contact with her child or the family, those photos were all she had of the little boy she had lost.

"So that's it?" I said. "Your mom won't give me any info?"

"She can't," Lynda said with a sigh. "It would be illegal. Plus, she doesn't want to betray a trust."

I fell into a despondent silence.

"You get that my mom's in a terrible position, right?"

I closed my eyes. "I guess."

But I couldn't deny I felt a new hole crowding the others in my heart. My half-brother was alive, as far as I knew, but in that moment, I felt that partially open door click shut and lock, that chance I thought I'd have to look into his eyes and tell him that I missed growing up with him . . . and that I loved him . . . thrown away with the key.

———

While I strived valiantly to push the notion of meeting my long-lost brother out of my daily thoughts, Bill had something else on his mind: that we bite the bullet and buy a house together. He had grown understandably tired of making the thirty-mile drive from my apartment to work multiple times a week, and since we were staying at each other's places for longer and longer stretches, living together in a more permanent way made sense.

Still, I was reluctant at first. Though I loved Bill deeply, my abandonment issues stepped boldly in front of that love to warn me that if things didn't work out between us, there would not only be a relationship cracked down the seam, but a home too. I had already been ripped from a relationship and the home that cradled it, however precariously, and it terrified me that I could face that all over again.

It took some convincing on Bill's part, but I finally acquiesced. Though our relationship was still young, it was solid, and I had every reason to believe it would continue to be. So while it wasn't an ideal location for either one of us, Riverside—an inland town about fifty miles from Laguna—was a city where we could buy a decent home for a relatively low investment. Bill was willing to continue commuting to his school in south Orange County, but I saw the move as an opportunity for change. So I gave my notice as head of the GATE program and prepared to find a position that would offer me a new challenge—and more money.

A friend in the district told me that the well-known academic publisher Houghton-Mifflin was looking for a sales rep. Back in my college days, I had worked at a few women's clothing shops—they didn't typically hire men at these stores, but I had always loved women's fashion and I got along great with the female staff. Helping the girls who shopped there was like dressing life-size Barbie dolls, and I not only enjoyed being the Bob Mackie of the mall, but I excelled as one of the top salespeople.

So, having relished the relative freedom I had in my last position, along with my penchant for sales, I jumped at the chance to interview for the open spot. As fate would have it, the interviewer asked to meet me in the lobby of the hotel where I used to work—the precise place where my former manager had covered for me while I scored hookers for guests—and while I pimped myself out on select nights.

"I'll be there," I confirmed, my stomach clenching at the irony.

During the interview, I found out that the position would require frequent travel, to the main office in New York as well as to multiple cities in what would be my assigned territory in California. I would have a company car and expense account, and I would get to talk to educated professionals every day, which I found appealing. We both saw the position as a perfect match for me. The level of autonomy was right, the salary was right. The guy even let me choose the color of my new company car. The only snag in the plan was that Bill wasn't so keen on being in a relationship where he would rarely see me. He made it clear that he would never hold me back from a great opportunity if I felt it was right for me, but that he couldn't promise he would stay in an essentially long-distance relationship for the long haul.

At that moment, my abandonment alarm went off. I loved Bill, and I couldn't bear the thought of pushing him to leave me because of a job. The prestige and increased salary simply weren't worth potentially losing the best man I'd ever met. So I turned the position down and applied for teaching positions in our nearby school district.

At the time, one of the high schools was looking for a psychology/home economics teacher, and an elementary school was searching for a kindergarten teacher. So I interviewed for both and got both. The high school job offered higher pay, but while I would have loved teaching psychology, the home ec part—despite being a good cook—wasn't really my thing. I figured I could wing it, but it didn't sit well with me. The more I thought about it, even though the pay was less, I was drawn to the kindergarten position. Perhaps I was also flattered by the fact that the district had never hired a man as a kindergarten teacher before, so that's the one I accepted.

This was way before Arnold Schwarzenegger tried to make a go of teaching five-year-olds in *Kindergarten Cop*, so I had no real frame of reference. But what I did have was my vivid memories of what being a kindergartner was like—the rigid rules, the consistent punishments for small infractions, the demand to stay quiet. In preschool, I had flourished in the structured yet carefree environment of working in learning centers for different subjects, and I figured I could incorporate the same idea for my students so that they could flourish too. I also imagined how wonderful it would be to give the children all the loving guidance and recognition I never received at that age.

On my first day of class, twenty-five faces that reminded me of myself as a little boy stared up at me in anticipation. *This is my chance to start their education in a positive way*, I thought. *I can't let them down.*

"Hello, everyone," I said with great enthusiasm. "Welcome to your first day of kindergarten!" I glanced around to see some of the children light up, while others remained encased in their reticence. "I'm Mr. Ecke." I paused for effect. "That sounds kind of like 'icky,' doesn't it?" I scrunched my face, and all the children burst out laughing, some with those exaggerated goofy laughs that children are so fond of, the kind of laughter that erupts when they feel trust and freedom in your presence. I smiled, relishing the connection I felt we had just made. "But I promise you, they'll be nothing icky about being in my class. We're going to have a lot of fun together."

The kids looked around at each other and smiled, as if whatever fears they were harboring had just magically disappeared.

Being the first male kindergarten teacher in the district, the administration kept a pretty close eye on me. But luckily for me, every time one of them popped into my classroom, the children were thriving in one of the learning centers, or rapt in a story I was reading them, or simply being children without turning the room into a circus. On the playground, instead of merely overseeing their play, I interacted with them, teaching them social skills and how to play fairly and nicely with each other. What was most fun, though, was joining them on the swings—they got a kick out of taking turns pushing me, and I would find myself drifting into dream mode just like I had when I was a child.

As rules went, I had simple ones the kids could grasp and follow with some gentle coaching. When someone didn't follow the rules, I took him aside and quietly explained the hurt he could—or did—cause by not respecting those rules. I never denigrated or punished a child for misbehaving; instead I strove to see inside her and tap into what needs weren't met for her. Using empathy in place of harsh discipline made my students some of the most well behaved, willingly compliant, and educationally competent in the entire school, and the principal recognized my efforts with awards—and a renewal of my contract for another year.

In the second year, the administration decided to capitalize on my abilities and increase my class size to nearly fifty. Most of the children were low-income boys, some of whom were labeled as gifted but had certain learning disabilities, exactly the way I did at that age. Though it was an enormous responsibility—and overwhelming prospect—to have so many five-year-olds in one room, I also saw the providence of all these little ones, especially boys I could relate to, being under my charge. If I could reach them, foster the talents they had while working in creative ways on the ones that didn't come so naturally, perhaps I could shift the trajectory of their education from potentially deflating to encouraging and empowering.

So, I accepted the challenge and made my classroom a veritable stage. I dressed up in costumes and pranced around the room as different characters in the books I read them, eliciting wide eyes and genuine emotion—laughter when the character was silly, sincere worry when he was in peril, tears if something tragic occurred, happiness when he prevailed. I put a sturdy box at the front of the room for show and tell, complete with a microphone, so that the children learned to be in the spotlight and cultivate strong speaking skills early on. When they showed their bravery and did well, they received standing ovations, which motivated the kids who were a bit more shy to project themselves better the next time. I never gave them more than they could handle individually, and I focused intently on providing all the fun activities and learning games I had missed at that age.

But perhaps my most embraced offering was the chance to earn points for good behavior, kind acts, and excellent work that they could trade for special treats—not candy or sweets, but opportunities that had meaning for them. Once they accumulated enough points, they had three choices for how they could spend them:

1. Be the teacher for an hour
2. Comb Mr. Ecke's hair
3. Give Mr. Ecke a back rub

I realize that on the surface, these choices may have seemed incredibly self-serving, even inappropriate. After all, being in physical contact with a teacher, especially a male one, wasn't particularly encouraged, or even tolerated. But I knew my kids better than any administrator ever could. Many of my boys were fatherless and were abused or neglected, and I felt every ounce of their angst and pain. Allowing them innocent physical contact with me afforded them a chance to bond in a way that made them feel valued; in fact, when given the choice, they almost always chose combing my hair or rubbing my back over being the teacher. Today, I likely would have been erroneously labeled a pedophile and fired for these benign reward sessions, but lucky for me—and for the children—no such action was ever taken against me. In contrast, my boys acted out less, showed more kindness, and grew a level of confidence that they might not have otherwise, all because they had the opportunity to connect with a male role model who believed in their inherent gifts and goodness.

My goal may have been to help heal them, but in being able to give the kids the very things I had missed, they also helped to heal me.

CHAPTER TWENTY-ONE

A s much as I loved teaching kindergarten, I was driven by my persistent desire to never stop reaching for more. My salary was pitifully low for the responsibility I carried, and I couldn't help but want a life with more pizzazz than we could afford. What's more, Bill and I hated living in Riverside. Though we had a nice home, the summers were like wearing a blanket over your head with a heater blowing underneath, the winters were colder than we preferred, and it was fifty traffic-laden miles to the beach, a drive that didn't take long not to relish in the least.

At that time, Laguna Beach had become more and more of a town that embraced the gay community. Though it was still prudent not to blatantly advertise your sexuality in society at large, there were plenty of same-sex couples and gay bars and clubs in Laguna to give a semblance of fitting in—for many people for the first time. Bill and I spent every weekend there and cultivated a diverse circle of friends. My father also owned a shop there, so while we weren't particularly close, it was another tie to the beautiful beach town we loved.

Ever the forward-looking, spontaneous creature that I was, I saw an ad one day for floral school and grasped on to the idea like a child with an outstretched hand in a toy aisle. I had been dabbling in flowers for a while, brightening up the teachers' lounge and even putting together a simple wedding for a colleague, but I had never studied floral arranging formally.

"Floral school?" Bill said when I proposed the idea. "Since when do you have an interest in that?"

"I've always loved flowers. And flowers are an art form. Plus, we have the whole summer coming . . . I just think it might be cool to check it out."

Bill had zero interest in attending floral school with me. He had just applied for law school and had a completely different career path planned. But he admired my adventurous side; he was also the biggest supporter of my creative ambitions. So, reluctantly agreeing to join me, we enrolled in the program and began to learn the basics. Before long, Bill was as enthusiastic about the whole endeavor as I was. In fact, he consistently received praise for his ability to create precisely what the teacher instructed, while I was constantly called out for putting too much "flair" into mine.

By the end of the course, Bill had made the decision not to attend law school after all. With his head for business and my creative vision, we could both see the possibilities of opening an innovative shop in mostly wealthy Laguna. But we couldn't simply leave our jobs, with little money in the bank, to embark on a new and risky business venture.

We had no idea that our dream would come alive with the help of an unexpected benefactor.

My father was a collector of antique Britains, painted lead military figures that were highly prized for their value because the majority of them had been melted for bullets during World War II. Over the years, my father had amassed the largest collection of these figures on the planet, and celebrities like Katharine Hepburn and Jonathan Winters would hang out in his shop to play "war games" with them, similar to a game of Risk. He became the foremost authority on these collectibles, which gave him the spotlight he always craved.

But despite the relative fame my father wore like a Miss Universe sash, puffing him out with pride, his health was declining. He was still married to Shirley, but he had lapsed back into his alcohol addiction and had his share of flings. Busy with her psychology practice and raising a daughter from her first husband, Shirley had allowed my dad a lot of freedom—too much freedom. But his ever-present charm hadn't faded despite his transgressions, and she still maintained her love for him, just like my mother had through the worst of times. When he proposed opening a shop to house and sell his vintage figures, she purchased the building in Laguna Beach, giving him something on which to focus his wandering eye—and to temper his physical exertion as his body began to fail him.

After seeing some of our work and recognizing our talent, he came to Bill and me with the proposition of taking over the front of his building. Knowing he didn't have much time left, and perhaps influenced by his guilt for not being around much for me growing up—as well as his current irrational fear that the war games he hosted had aroused the suspicion of government officials who were somehow "watching" him—he thought the arrangement would be a perfect one. Thrilled by his offer, we agreed. He wasn't strong enough physically to participate in the move, but he looked on with a gratified smile as Shirley, Bill, and I carefully transported his collectibles to the more clandestine section in the back of the building, where he could fraternize with his celebrity friends away from spying eyes, and we could situate a flower shop in the front.

Juggling our teaching jobs with opening the shop proved to be a challenge, but one that was marked by anticipation akin to waiting for Santa on Christmas Eve. Like a boy pumping with all his might on the playground swings, each swoop backward was maintaining our jobs and routine in Riverside, and each swoop upward was tying a bow on our new business in Laguna. Both directions carried their own exhilaration, but once the swing slowed to a stop, we were fittingly facing forward, ready to rush with the spark of youthful abandon into our new life.

———

The Black Iris opened in mid-December, and though our first Christmas season was relatively short, it exceeded our modest expectations. Applying my artistic inspiration, we specialized in not just typical arrangements and bouquets, but in works of floral art unlike our customers had ever seen. I also embraced the opportunity to put my display skills to work that I'd honed back in my retail days, when I was promoted to the position of visual merchandiser after management was impressed by my window displays.

With no one to dictate parameters of what I could do—and it being the holiday season—I began what would become an annual tradition of showcasing several towering Christmas trees inside our front windows, each one decorated in a unique and lavish theme that veered from the norm. The trees drew customers in the door, and the distinct arrangements that greeted them once inside, along with the beautiful gifts sprinkled throughout, surprised and delighted them. Word seemed to spread quickly that we were the new innovative trendsetter in town, and I reveled not only in the creative expression, but in the feeling of moving toward an exciting new chapter in our lives.

The day after Christmas, celebrating both Bill's birthday and how the community had embraced our shop, we were toasting our goal of taking leaves of absence from our teaching jobs within the next two years when we received a call from Shirley. My father, riddled with advanced liver disease and succumbing to congestive heart failure, had passed away at the age of forty-nine.

CHAPTER TWENTY-TWO

It is a bewildering dichotomy to find yourself at once a grown man and an orphan. The adult in me was savoring the dreams that were, one by one, beginning to come true: sharing my life with a man of utmost character, sensitivity, intellect, and caring; relishing my time near the beach when I was at the shop; transitioning my career into a business that was our own to grow like a distinct garden of thoughtfully chosen blooms. But the child in me had been dropped off at the Fletchers all over again—only this time, there were no weekend visitations, no kisses to look forward to from my mother, no hope of all of us being a happy family again. I may have been safely nestled in my relationship with Bill, but the abandonment I felt was as raw as when I was four.

———

Shortly after my father died, Shirley abruptly decided that our use of the building rent-free for the shop was no longer acceptable. Reneging on my father's agreement with us, she demanded that we start paying rent immediately or get out. I was shocked, not only because Shirley had always been so kind to me, but because my father, not having made a will, automatically left everything to Shirley and nothing to his children. It would have been an honorable gesture to allow us to at least build the business longer before changing our arrangement, but she left us no choice but to buy the entire property. Unable to afford both our house and the building, we were forced to make a tough decision.

Above the shop were three small apartments that had fallen into disrepair. Though our dreams had never included living in a Dickens' novel, Bill and I sold our house and moved into one of the upstairs rooms. Committed to saving money and growing the business, we grudgingly dropped ourselves into a space desperately in need of a remodel and made living in a veritable lap of no luxury our motivation to succeed as quickly as possible.

After the flurry of that first holiday season died down, we quickly returned to being the new kid on the block. Any other business would likely have struggled; advertising was expensive and out of reach, and being a destination shop, not everyone knew we even existed yet. But if ever two people had an angel, it was Bill and me.

Carol was a classy and beautiful interior designer who was the cousin of a male friend of mine. He arranged for us to meet, thinking our creativity in common might make for a nice connection—and he was right. Carol fell in love with us and we with her immediately. She hired us to create some unique arrangements and party decorations for her upper-class friends and clients, and when the feedback was positive, she hired us to do more. When she found out about my father's offer to share his building and open the shop, she was our loudest cheerleader, making us believe that with talent like ours, we couldn't fail. After we shared the news with her that we were going for it, she flashed one of her broad, winning smiles and gave us her blessing. She also took us under her wing for some much-needed education.

Carol had decorated the homes of some of the biggest names and socialites, and she and her husband shared a sizable combined wealth. Far from snobbish herself, she knew how far upward other rich people's noses could point, and she knew us well enough to know that we had never really dabbled in their world. So, knowing we were going to be opening an upscale shop in the middle of mostly affluent Laguna, she began teaching us about the material things wealthy people cared about so we wouldn't be rendered dumbstruck at the mention of names like Lladro, Lalique, Lenox, and Baccarat. As she polished our understanding of the finer things, she also taught us how to speak to wealthy clients, and how to appease and please them. By the time the shop opened, we felt like we had effectively been the Eliza Doolittles to her Henry Higgins in *My Fair Lady*.

After the first New Year of our business dawned, we began receiving ten to twenty-five orders a week to deliver elaborate arrangements to Carol's friends and clients in the area. She claimed that if she was going to send them flowers, she wanted to send the finest. But the truth was that Carol knew how important a reliable influx of business would mean for us financially. For the first year we were open, every person in Carol's address book must have received at least a dozen arrangements from The Black Iris.

One day, Carol came down to the shop for a visit. She wanted a tour, so we showed her around downstairs, then took to her up to the dilapidated upstairs' rooms. We could see that she felt for the one that was ours, but she also didn't want to hurt whatever amount of pride we may have had.

"I have an idea," she said, twirling around to face us. "The one apartment, farthest from yours, would make a lovely getaway retreat for me and my friends. I'd like to invest, say, a hundred thousand dollars in remodeling it for that purpose, and then when we're not here, you can use it as a suite for your bridal consults. What do you think?"

Bill and I looked at each other speechless, then back at Carol. "That would be fine with us," Bill said. "But that's an awful lot. Are you sure it's worth it for you?"

"Oh absolutely," Carol said. "With my designer's eye, it'll be a great project for me . . . and I'll make it a really lovely space for your customers. Unless," she hesitated, "it would feel a little too close for comfort for you two."

Bill and I stole glances at each other again. We could read in our expressions that neither of us was concerned. We would still have our privacy, and it would be a definite improvement to the overall property. Plus, we certainly didn't plan to live there long term if we didn't have to.

"If that's what you want to do . . ." I said.

Carol raised her shoulders and clapped her hands together like an excited schoolgirl. "Oh! It's going to be so much fun!" Then she added, "On one condition."

"What's that?" I asked.

"That you don't see it until it's finished."

Bill smiled. "Well, we completely trust you. So it's a deal!"

———

After a few months of contractors coming and going, and Carol working her magic, Carol rapped on our apartment door.

"It's time!" she shrieked. "The suite's ready for its unveiling."

Barely able to contain her enthusiasm, she grabbed our hands and walked us to the apartment. Carefully, as if unwrapping a gift, she opened the door with a "ta-da!"

Bill's and my mouths dropped open. Sunlight beamed through the windows to reveal a veritable fairy tale. The suite boasted white textured wallpaper with framed pastel paintings to break up the starkness, blush brocade drapes, and smooth white couches. A classy glass chandelier hung down from the middle of the ceiling, spraying sparkles of dancing light onto each surface. White antique-style tables and Queen Anne chairs upholstered in a soft floral print framed a sitting area, with blush-colored lamps and feminine touches of candles and tasteful trinkets peppered throughout. Bridal magazines were fanned across the coffee table like colorful invitations, with crystal candy dishes filled with Jordan almonds and butter mints flanking either end.

Bill and I looked at each other awe-struck, our faces betraying the feeling that we'd just won the grand prize on a popular game show.

"Oh my God," I exclaimed, "Carol! This is beyond gorgeous! You've completely outdone yourself!"

Carol beamed. "Well . . . I'm the one who really got to have all the fun." She winked. "So you approve?"

"Yes!" Bill and I blurted out at once, soaking in the impressive result of the six figures she had invested.

"Now," she said, pulling us both to the couch and sitting down opposite us. "Since this is technically your space, I propose paying you a thousand dollars a month rent. I think that should cover it when my friends or I stay here. How does that sound to you?"

"But Carol," Bill said. "You just put all this money into it . . . I hardly think—"

"Oh now," Carol said with a wave of her hand. "You don't worry about that. What's important to me is that you're fairly compensated when we use the space."

Bill and I were rendered silent.

"So it's settled then," Carol announced, not waiting for us to produce a response. She popped up from her chair and squeezed between us. "How wonderful," she said, turning to each of us and draping her arms over our shoulders. "Now I have a getaway retreat and you have a bridal suite. We both win!"

———

Over the next five years, Carol and her friends used the suite as their getaway retreat a grand total of three times.

She never missed sending us the monthly thousand-dollar checks. And we never missed an opportunity to acknowledge her as our living angel.

CHAPTER TWENTY-THREE

1981

With Carol's ever-present support, both emotionally and financially, we had begun to make our mark and actually turn some profit, which was rare for a business in its first year. Both Bill and I recognized that we'd been given a once-in-a-lifetime hand up with Carol, and we were committed to working as hard as we could to make her faith and monetary investment in us worthwhile.

In The Black Iris's second year, while Bill kept his job with the district, I took a leave of absence from my teaching position. Running the shop full-time, I became even more focused on attracting creative, artistic people to work for us who hadn't been formally trained in the floral arts. Some knowledge of flowers was a must, but I didn't want anyone who was steeped in traditional techniques—the less they had been "indoctrinated," the more open they were to my outside-the-box methods, and the more they embraced my requirement of making every arrangement that went out our door a one-of-a-kind achievement.

To me, floral arranging wasn't just about making the elements look pleasing; it was a responsibility to make each flower dance with another. Our signature style, which was both tropical and exotic, demanded that positioning was key, and that everything that accompanied the flowers came from nature—such as sticks or dramatic sprigs of greenery—as well as make a statement. Each arrangement sat in a fashionable architectural container, giving it the distinction of an unrepeated contemporary piece of art.

Although we were beginning to cultivate a clientele for our avant-garde creations, we hadn't yet reached the mainstream. For some, we were simply too far removed from tradition; for others, our exotic flowers were too expensive. We had no idea that another serendipitous turn was about to change all that, taking our ground-level revenue to penthouse-level in a matter of weeks.

Eschbach's, a premiere florist across town where everyone who was anyone purchased old-world bouquets and arrangements, had been serving our community for decades. Mr. Eschbach was not only highly respected in Laguna, but internationally, and when he died after an illness, his family was notably overwhelmed. In the midst of their grief and the myriad arrangements to make, they couldn't handle the onslaught of orders that poured in from their customers, many of them for the funeral or for the family itself. So, in an act of both self-preservation and good will, his parents and sister closed the doors and sent the majority of their business to The Black Iris.

In an instant, the shop was flooded with orders. As each batch went out the door, another one seemed to come in. Eschbach customers were incredibly loyal, so having the family endorse us as a recommended shop was like announcing to a thousand children that Santa—the most trusted icon in kid-lore—had just arrived and was awaiting them around the corner. The beeline to our door was swift, and Eschbach customers who hadn't known we existed, or wouldn't have dared go elsewhere, suddenly became dedicated clients.

Before long, word spread about our specialty designs, and we began using our posh bridal suite to meet with high-profile customers like the Pillsburys and the Nixons, who were throwing lavish weddings for their daughters, and Elizabeth Taylor, who was hoping to marry her soul mate once and for all in wedding number seven. Celebrities like Ozzie and Harriet Nelson and O.J. and Nicole Simpson hired us to create elaborate floral decorations for their socialite soirées, and corporations such as Pier 1 and Pepsi engaged us to put their company parties over the top. Each high-profile event seemed to merit a writeup in a newspaper or magazine; invitations to charity galas poured in, where we would attend in black tie and donate the flowers. As we became recognized in all of the social circles, we not only made scores of friends and admired associates, but we were able to upgrade our lives—starting with our apartment.

Bill and I had dreams of one day building a custom home, so after he left his teaching job in 1982, we were determined not to be too frivolous with our newfound cashflow from the shop. So, instead of moving to a nicer condo, we remodeled our upstairs apartment from dumpster drab to contemporary classy. It wasn't our dream home, but we did feel a bit like The Jeffersons as they moved on up.

––––––

Despite the wonderful new life we were building, one persistent inner battle never ceased to assault me: the conflict I felt over my sexuality. It was still widely believed that anyone who wasn't "straight" had some sort of mental illness, one that required severe intervention, such as shock therapy, to curtail. My mother had endured shock therapy and it had only made her worse, and I had already suffered through weeks of aversion therapy that hadn't changed me in the least. All of it left me horribly confused, and even afraid. Mental illness ran in my family, so who was to say I didn't inherit it, and that my errant sexuality was how it manifested in me?

To complicate my feelings further, the gay community had begun openly protesting more for civil rights, but I had remained behind the scenes, afraid to assert myself in that way in public. I felt like a coward and a traitor for not speaking up and joining the voices of my comrades; years earlier I had reasoned that I didn't want to jeopardize my teaching career, which was true—but that was now over. The truth was that the fear went deeper than that.

Even though I had lived with Dan for five years, and I was now living with Bill and running a business with him, I still assumed that no one in my family knew I was gay. I had kept it from both my parents until the day they died, and I believed my sisters thought the men in my life were merely close friends of mine, or in Bill's case, my business partner. No one ever inquired—presumably because they didn't want to have to acknowledge or accept an unfavorable answer—and I never volunteered otherwise.

Until one weekend, when Noel came over to visit our upgraded digs.

With me out of earshot, Noel approached Bill and gingerly put her hand on his arm. Out of the blue, she asked, "Is Paul gay?"

Bill, taken aback, and knowing my position with my family, merely smiled. "Well, *I'm* gay. But you'll have to ask him if *he* is."

Noel tipped her head with a grin, conceding to play the game. She ambled into the adjacent room and up to me. "Paul," she said gently.

I turned to face her.

She paused for a moment and stared into my eyes. "Are you gay?"

My heart jumped as I bit my lip and glanced away.

"You can tell me," she assured me.

Of all my sisters, Noel was the first to ever ask—and to seemingly care. But I couldn't bear the thought of what she would think of me if she knew the truth. I had managed what I believed was a brilliant façade my entire life, and I had grown accustomed to it within my family. Recently, that façade had morphed into a full-on dual existence. At the charity galas and celebrity weddings, it was almost expected that the floral designer be stereotypically flamboyant, and I played that role to project an air of artistry and creativity, seemingly to the audience's acceptance. To abruptly pull down the proverbial curtain with my sister unnerved me. But I saw the tenderness with which Noel was looking at me, and something inside me shifted.

"Yes," I confessed. "I am." My eyes involuntarily filled with tears. "I hope that won't change how you feel about me."

Noel took my face in her hands as hers softened even more. "I love you just the way you are," she said. "Nothing will ever change that."

With a relief that washed over me like a soothing ocean wave, I hugged my youngest sister to me. A part of me felt like a child letting go of his mother's hand, with her permission to run unbound down the sandy stretch before him, the salty breeze kissing every inch of his face, as a small piece of him was set free. Yet another felt the opaque bubble of perceived security I'd been floating in become transparent, unsettling and exposing me with a level of vulnerability that made me want to fold myself into my mother's skirt as I had when I was a boy.

CHAPTER TWENTY-FOUR

After another remodel in 1985, The Black Iris had become the premiere flower shop in Southern California, not only for bouquets and unique arrangements, but for worldly gifts as well. Taking inspiration from fine stores such as Gump's and Harrod's, along with European influence, we converted the final upstairs apartment into a luxurious gift shop and filled it with treasures from high-end vendors and the world travels the shop's profits had afforded us. A talented landscape architect, using our own design conceptions, fashioned gorgeous gardens on the property with distinctive outdoor art for sale. Each holiday season drew hundreds of people to our "living windows," which were my signature annual creation, and business was booming like never before. Everything we created had meaning and a theme, and with ongoing requests for weekly arrangements and party décor, we now housed a home design staff to work with our regulars.

We had also moved out of our upstairs apartment and into a modest condo near the shop across from the ocean. It had been overwhelming to have our home and work lives be so intertwined, and the move gave us a much-needed division between the two.

It seemed that the particles of the prosperous life I had visualized as a boy had come together in a sort of dance of the tangible, and Bill's and my relationship was stronger than ever. But underlying it all was a shard from my past poking at me from inside, urging me to find answers.

It had been twelve years since I found the photos of the little boy in my mother's wallet after she died, eleven since Lynda's mother, Edna, said she could do nothing to help me find my brother. I had decided to wait until he turned twenty-one to pursue it any further, but that time had come and gone, lost in a blur of years working a nearly 24/7 schedule of parties, benefits, and running a thriving business. Now, however, that smoldering ember sparked, and I figured it couldn't hurt to ask.

Sitting across from Edna, she sighed uncomfortably and looked away for a few moments.

"Come on, Mom," Lynda pleaded on my behalf. "This really means a lot to Paul."

When Edna returned her eyes to mine, she said, "Okay. I'll tell you his name. But that's it. And you have to swear that if you find him, no one will know I was involved."

I nodded swiftly and threw my arms around her. "Thank you so much. I won't let this come back to haunt you, I promise."

When I pulled away, she said, "His name is Evan Robertson."

Armed with all I needed to track down the young man I so longed to meet, I hired a private detective. Within a week, she told me she had found my brother, and that he worked in a family pizza restaurant only miles from our condo.

Elated with the prospect of seeing Evan in person, I convinced Bill to go to the restaurant for dinner one night. I had my reservations about being seen as a couple, though, so I invited one of our woman friends along for balance.

After we arrived and were seated, I immediately spotted Evan. Though he hadn't inherited the short stature of my parents and siblings, and he had curly hair, not straight, like my uncle, I could see the resemblance to us in his face. When it turned out that he was our server, it took everything in me to nonchalantly play first-time customer, not long-lost brother he probably knew nothing about.

The pizza was delicious, but its satisfaction paled in comparison to being in close proximity to the baby brother I believed for years had died. Preoccupied the entire meal, I only half listened to the conversation Bill and our friend were having. All I could think about was one thing: how I could move from being just another patron to being a family member without upending Evan's world.

After visiting the restaurant five more times, a couple of which Evan was our server again, he recognized us and we became friendly, sharing innocent small talk. But I knew this charade couldn't go on indefinitely, plus I wanted to know Evan as my brother, not in a casual way as a server. So I decided it was time to let him know that I wasn't merely a customer, but someone much more significant, I hoped.

When we arrived home that night after dinner, I called the restaurant and asked for Evan. When he got on the phone, I described myself, reminding him that we'd just eaten there.

"Oh yeah," he said. "I know who you are. Did you leave something behind?"

I paused. "No . . . actually . . . there's something I need to tell you. Something you're probably going to be surprised to hear."

"Oh?" he said, sounding anxious.

I took a deep breath. "Evan, I'm sure you know you were adopted. But what you probably don't know is that you have four siblings from your biological mother. Three sisters and . . . me. I'm your brother."

There was silence on the other end, then, "Uh . . . I'm sorry, man," he said. "But you must have me confused with someone else. I wasn't adopted."

My mouth dropped slightly open and I pulled back, finding it hard to believe he could have been on the planet for twenty-six years, with an Asian mother and no trace of Asian in him, without a clue that he'd been adopted. I knew I needed to tread lightly, though. If he was telling the truth, I was dropping a bigger bomb on him than I imagined.

"I . . . I'm really sorry if this is news to you. But I know you're the right person. I don't mean to dump it on you like this, but I can't keep coming into the restaurant and pretending. I've wanted to meet you my whole life."

A longer, more uncomfortable silence met me this time. "Look," he finally said, "I'm at work. I can't talk to you about this right now."

My heart was pounding. "I understand. I'll let you go. But will you at least write down my phone number? When you're ready to talk, I'll be here."

Evan agreed to take my number, though I had no idea if he actually wrote it down, then we hung up with an awkward good-bye.

Bill was staring at me, his bright blue eyes conveying his compassion. "Oh, honey . . . are you okay? It sounded like maybe he's in denial."

I shook my head. "Not just that . . . he claims he doesn't know he was adopted."

"What? How's that possible?"

"I don't know. But that's what he said."

"Did he say he'd call you?"

I shrugged. "I think he wrote down our number. But I honestly don't know if he'll ever call."

Bill came and wrapped me in his arms. "I know this isn't the initial reaction you wanted, babe. But give him some time. He may come around."

A tear fell onto Bill's shoulder. "Yeah," I said. "Maybe."

———

A couple months later, the phone rang. When I answered, an unfamiliar voice said, "Hi, is this Paul?"

"Yes," I confirmed.

He paused. "It's Evan."

My heart leapt. "Hey. How are you?"

He gave a half laugh. "I don't know how I am."

I paused, feeling guilty. "I guess not, huh?"

"That was a pretty big bomb you dumped on me. I really didn't know I was adopted until you told me."

"Shit," I said. "I'm sorry about that. I honestly thought you'd know. Everyone I've ever known who was adopted has known practically their whole life. I just assumed . . ."

"Yeah . . . well, you assumed wrong."

I apologized again, hoping I hadn't blown our chances of getting to know each other.

"Look," he said. "I don't want my parents knowing I'm in touch with you, okay? They'd be pretty upset. But I'm willing to meet . . . somewhere . . . and at least find out how all this happened."

I smiled wide. "That's wonderful." I glanced at a calendar. "Is this weekend too soon?"

The following Saturday, Evan and I met at a small café, between his restaurant and The Black Iris, where it was unlikely anyone would recognize either of us. When we sat down, he seemed less resentful and more curious, so I spilled the entire story—about our parents' dysfunctional marriage, the sister they had given up years earlier, our mother's emotional issues and affair with our uncle, our father's anger over the pregnancy, our mother telling us Evan had died to protect our feelings.

"Damn," he said. "You actually thought I was dead all those years?"

I nodded. "But please don't blame our mother for that. I was pretty upset too when I found out she'd lied to us, but I get why she did it. It was pretty intense to know one sister was adopted out. She must have thought it would be too much for us to know they did that twice."

"I guess."

We both stirred our potato salad around.

"So," I ventured, unsure how to shift the conversation into a more lighthearted topic, "have you had a good life?"

He laughed. "Sure. My parents are great. I grew up in a nice house with nice things. And I have a sister . . . who, by the way, didn't know she was adopted either."

I held in my shock and tried to substitute it with something less mocking. "Wow. Really? So you told her?"

"Yeah. She was pretty shaken up about it."

I leaned in slightly and lowered my voice. "But . . . I don't understand. I thought your mother was Asian."

"She is," Evan said matter-of-factly, taking a bite of his sandwich.

"So . . . didn't you ever wonder why you didn't have any Asian traits?"

He shrugged. "I don't know. Sometimes the Asian is pretty watered down. My dad is tall and dark like me. I don't have their features so much, but I figured I maybe took after a relative or something. I don't look *that* different from my dad."

I was still dumbstruck, but I strove not to show it. "Hmm. And I guess they didn't want you to know . . . or they would have told you a long time ago."

"I guess. My parents are very protective. If they knew I had a bunch of siblings, they probably thought I'd want to meet them some-day. And they'd feel threatened by that."

A nod was all I could muster.

"So they can't know we've met, okay? I don't like keeping this from them, but I don't have a choice."

I nodded again. "I get it."

But I wondered if I really did.

———

Shortly after our first meeting, I asked Evan if I could take him to meet our sisters. He agreed, though a bit reluctantly, so I took it slow: first Tina, then Noel, then Gail, all on different days. Though he seemed intrigued to meet all of us, and we had great conversation each time, I could tell he wasn't completely comfortable. I wasn't sure if it was the lying to his parents or something more he wasn't saying, but I couldn't help but think that perhaps my dream of having a brother at last was going to be as short lived as the weekend visits with my mother at the Fletchers'.

CHAPTER TWENTY-FIVE

Tentative at best, though I continued to pursue it, my relationship with Evan wasn't what I hoped it would be. What's more, after ten years of running The Black Iris with Bill, my persistent perfectionism and anxiety had morphed into full-blown OCD. I was driving myself—and the people around me—crazy; I was hard on the staff I didn't deem up to par, and I had to approve every piece that went out the door. Despite paying well and providing great benefits, several of our best designers ended up leaving to open up their own shops. The grind of the intense training of new designers put me over my persnickety edge, and I knew only an outside person could help me.

So I started seeing a cognitive therapist.

It was slow at first, but working through the various exercises she gave me, I learned to focus more on the here and now and less on the subconscious things that affected me from my past. Though my abandonment issues were never far from the surface, I wasn't one to dwell consciously on the pain from my childhood; in fact, I always strove to focus on the positive over the negative. But she helped me understand that unresolved issues were likely affecting me nonetheless. My perfectionist ways, especially at the shop, were a means of proving my worth, and she brought to light that they sometimes more avidly projected a desire to control. That led me to a humbling aha moment: not everyone could be me in the sense of my high expectations—but that others could, in fact, be even *better* than me at what I did. Over the months, the activities she prescribed helped me find a greater sense of calm, and I actually felt I might be claiming stronger control of my emotional self.

Until one of our "uptown" clients pushed the wrong button with me.

I had spent years cultivating warm relationships with the privileged class we mostly served, and despite the arrogance of some, I learned to get along well with the majority. One day, however, one of our clients took her sense of privilege too far.

She had ordered two matching wreaths, and being that both were composed of varying elements of nature, there was no way the pair was going to look identical. But when I brought the wreaths out to her the day she came to pick them up, she started nitpicking the small differences between them, as if two flowers, or sticks, or vines, or leaves could look exactly alike.

"The symmetry's off," she scoffed. "I want you to make it more symmetrical."

I held my tongue. "But this is really the most symmetrical we can get with nature."

She wasn't convinced. "No," she insisted, "I want you to find pieces that look more alike to replace these with."

"But Mrs—"

"No buts, Paul. I want you to fix it."

That did it.

Something in me snapped. I looked at her and felt my face burning. When my mouth opened, there was no stopping the words, or the highly annoyed tone with which I said them.

"The only way you could get *more* symmetrical is to have *God* make them himself."

Her eyes widened. "How dare you speak to me like that!"

"Really?" I said, raising my voice. "How dare *you*."

She looked as though I had just slapped her across the face.

I hesitated a moment, then I walked over to the cooler, slid open the door, and pulled out a single red rose. I walked calmly back and handed it to her. "You'll never be satisfied," I said, "so it's probably best if you just leave."

Her eyes grew wide.

"And," I added as my final punctuation mark, "don't let the door hit you on the ass."

What I remember after that was the commotion of her leaving in a huff, the murmurs of the crowd in the shop, and a grasp of my arm that led me to the back room.

"What were you thinking talking to her like that?" Bill asked, his eyes frantic.

"She pissed me off. 'Make it more matching,'" I mocked. "Give me a fucking break. They're wreaths, not matching dresses!"

"Okay," Bill said calmly, "I get it, but—"

"I'm done," I said.

"What do you mean 'done'?"

"I'm not doing this anymore. I'm done."

Bill stared at me, seeming to process in an instant all the reasons it was time. Finally, he nodded.

"Okay," he said, resolute.

"Good," I said, equally resolute.

And that was the last time I ever stepped foot in The Black Iris.

With my newfound freedom, I needed something to occupy my time, and Bill suggested I use the empty warehouse we owned adjacent to the store to pursue my art. He knew I'd been suppressing the urge because all my time the last ten-plus years had been spent in the shop as a designer, or in some capacity related to it. So he told me to buy canvases, paint, whatever I needed, and discover another side of my artist's soul.

Embracing the opportunity, I took him up on it. It didn't take long to relish the big empty space to myself, with no employees to hover over, no customers to appease. I missed working with the flowers, but being surrounded by blank canvases was the grandest invitation to express my creativity; knowing they were waiting for me to transform them provided a consistent flow of inspiration.

Within a week or two of my abdication, I had a handful of paintings staring back at me, and I almost felt their kinship as if I was a member of a mutual admiration society. I quickly fell in love with my secluded workspace where no one bothered me, and I realized that for the first time maybe ever, I felt a sense of relief that I was no longer responsible to keep everyone in the shop humming at my level of perfectionism. I was pretty certain, too, that I wasn't the only one who was relieved.

One day, I was in the midst of my paint-splattered bliss when a woman's voice pierced my reverie.

"Well, *there* you are!"

I turned to see one of our regulars poking her head through the doorway, her hair-sprayed coif backlit by the sun.

"I asked for you and one of your employees said you were out here." She tentatively squeezed through and glided forward in her three-inch heels as she looked around approvingly—or was it disapprovingly? I thought to say no one was supposed to send customers out there, but before I could say a word, she pointed and exclaimed with seeming admiration, "Did you do these?"

I watched her as she hastened over to one. "Uh huh," I said casually.

She tipped her head to the side. "Hmm, I *really* like this one in particular." She spun around like a top to face me. "How much you want for it?"

My mouth dropped open slightly. "I . . . hadn't thought about it. They're not really for sale."

"Not for sale? Oh, come on. These are gorgeous! Give me a number."

I thought for a moment. "Three thousand?"

"Deal."

Though I had no intention of selling my first pieces of art from the warehouse, that first buyer told her socialite friends, who told their friends . . . and well, you get the picture. Soon I had ladies parading through my "studio" and offering me money for my paintings—ladies with big art collections and a discerning eye.

It wasn't a bad beginning by any means, but selling my paintings from four concrete walls and a matching floor wasn't exactly what I had in mind. If I was going to garner any attention of note, I knew it was important that I be featured in galleries or shows.

Having no real contacts in the art world yet, I needed an agent.

And I knew the perfect person to step into the role. He was polished and personable and everybody loved talking to him, so I thought he'd be the ideal representative of my art. It didn't matter that art wasn't his background; his personality would get a foot in the door, and my work would hopefully speak for itself once there.

"Are you serious?" Bill said when I proposed the idea. "You want me to just waltz into galleries and pitch your work?"

"Well, yeah. Why not? No one has to know we're a couple."

"I wasn't even thinking about that. I was just wondering how it would seem for me to present myself as your agent when I've never done anything like that before."

I smiled. "Honey. I've never met someone who wasn't enamored with you. Your charm is exactly what I need to open some doors for my work."

Bill rolled his eyes.

"Will you at least consider it?" I pleaded.

Bill grinned in spite of himself. "Okay. I'll think about it."

———

An artist can struggle for years to get a showing. But Bill strides into one art gallery in La Jolla and bam! I'm in.

Though it was a dark period in our nation—we were embroiled in the Gulf War and people didn't tend to spend money frivolously—somehow, the men and women who came into that gallery were not only drawn to my art, but they bought it. The gallery originally commissioned ten or so paintings, and I thought I would be lucky if half of those sold. But it didn't take long before they commissioned more. And then more. Before that year was over, I had sold fifty-four paintings, which was practically unheard of for an unknown like me, especially in the current economy.

Hailed as "hot," I was written up in the *LA Times*. Riding the wave of my newfound attention, we reinvested our profits in magazine ads to gain exposure, and other gallery opportunities started landing in my lap.

———

During this time, Bill and I had romanced the idea of building a home on the beautiful lot that sat across the street from our condo. It had been deemed "unbuildable land," but that didn't stop us from sitting on its earthen floor for hours at a time, imagining our dream house coming to life as we plotted out the rooms and envisioned the gardens and mentally stared out the windows that would face the lulling waves of the Pacific.

Believing there was no other spot that could suit us as perfectly as that one, we called upon various architects, but all of them said it simply couldn't be done. When we finally consulted with an architect who thought he could manage it with intense prep of the land beforehand, we rushed to buy the property. But within months, that first architect bowed out.

We were bleeding money at that point, but we were desperate. So when another architect stepped up and took the job, Bill worked alongside him for nearly a year to ensure there would be no snags.

Filled with hope, we watched the house from our condo's living room being painstakingly built. But at each turn, we faced another problem with water or pipes or land that couldn't be engineered properly. After another year passed, we couldn't help but wonder if those early architects had been right all along, and that we were sitting on nothing but a money pit that would rob us of our financial security and suck our dreams down with it.

CHAPTER TWENTY-SIX

1992

Two years into our house being built also marked two years that Evan and I had been reunited. I had seen him only eight or ten times, each time feeling him pull away more than the last. Eventually, he confessed to his parents that I had found him, and as suspected, they weren't happy. Over time, I believe he felt more and more conflicted over being connected with us, knowing it upset his family. It was also clear that we had come from two distinct worlds, which didn't allow us to connect on the same level. Still, we saw each other occasionally. I tried to be a mentor to him in business, and Bill and I even attended his wedding, albeit in the back row of the church and relegated to a nearly hidden corner of the reception.

The years of anticipation leading up to finding Evan, and not bonding like brothers the way I had dreamed, admittedly took a toll on me emotionally. I couldn't blame him; the situation was bizarre on both sides, but it filled me with sadness nonetheless.

One evening, Bill and I returned home from dinner to find a message on our answering machine.

"Hi. You don't know me, but my name's Ralph Hill. My wife is Laura . . . she was adopted and I think you may be her brother. Please call me if you're willing to talk . . ."

I turned to Bill with a look that said, *Oh my God.*

The next morning, I called the number Ralph had left and he answered. It didn't take long to determine that I was, indeed, Laura's brother. But before I imagined going down another complicated road with Laura the way I had with Evan, Ralph told me that Laura's adoptive parents were incredibly open and supportive of Laura reuniting with her family. Because they had essentially been her foster parents for a year before my parents relinquished their rights to her, they knew the story of our family, and that Laura had full-blood siblings.

All of Laura's life, despite her family's open invitation to know about her birth family, she hadn't been interested in finding us. But after she had children, her curiosity about her biological heritage shifted. When she shared her interest with her parents, they happily gave her her family name and told her she was born in Orange County. Living only thirty miles away in Long Beach, it was easy to open up the phone book and find a lone Ecke—not only is it an unusual last name, but being the only boy, and the girls all being married, I was the one sibling who still carried it.

When Ralph put Laura on the phone, it was surreal—she sounded so much like my sisters. Though it was a little awkward at first, we fell into nice conversation as we got to know each other, and she expressed that she was looking forward to meeting all of us. After we got off the phone, I called the girls, who were all stunned and elated, and within days we had arranged for everyone to meet at our condo where we could feel somewhat at home as a newly united family.

Meeting Laura proved to be a completely different experience from meeting Evan. Nothing clandestine or shameful hung over our reunion, and although it was expectedly overwhelming for all of us, it was also remarkable. Everything about Laura's physical appearance made her a dead ringer for our sister. She was short like us, had our brown hair and same facial features, and even had blue eyes like Gail. The girls laughed at how they had all inherited the large breasts of the women in our family, and how they relished having naturally tan skin. We sat comparing our hands and feet like little kids on a playground, in disbelief of how they were like matching sets. We also couldn't help but marvel at the strength of nature over nurture: Laura's gestures were amazingly like Tina's; her voice and the cadence of her speech, eerily similar to mine.

We spent the entire afternoon and early evening drinking wine, exchanging stories, and sharing photos. Above the decibels of the Ecke family's signature loudness, and in light of the tragic family story she learned from our side, it was difficult to tell if Laura believed she had dodged a bullet being given up for adoption, or if she wished she'd been a part of us all along.

———

The second time we got together with Laura, it was at her house with everyone's spouses and children in tow. Even Evan came. I quickly noticed how the girls—who mostly had exuberant personalities—had all married quieter men, and the guys immediately clicked. Laura s daughter and son were nine and six, and she had a twenty-three-year-old stepdaughter who floated between playing with her sister, brother, and Tina's son who was almost three, and hanging out getting to know the rest of us. Bill and I were the neutral couple, so we enjoyed being social with everyone. Maybe best of all was that it was impossible not to observe the light that clearly shown on everyone's faces. I couldn't help but wonder if my parents were present, with all the hurt and shame and resentment evaporated, smiling down on us as they saw all their children and their families together for the first time.

CHAPTER TWENTY-SEVEN

After four grueling, cash-devouring years—with more fits and starts than Spielberg endured with the mechanical shark in *Jaws*—the house that we had envisioned for so long as mere particles of our future was finally the Italian/contemporary reality we had dreamed of.

With my art career on the rise, I had longed to have a studio in our home. So it was a celebrated day when I moved all of my paints, brushes, canvases, and easels from the warehouse into my new lower-level studio, complete with twenty-foot ceilings and equally tall windows that allowed the aqueous blues, greens, and even intermittent browns of my treasured ocean view to playfully remind me that I was exactly where I was meant to be.

The studio became not only the space I painted in, but also where I hung out even when I wasn't painting. I was so at peace being awash in natural light, with the sound of the waves rolling and crashing, rolling and crashing, that I couldn't imagine anything more soothing to the soul. The studio became my sanctuary where I sipped glasses of wine and read art books, worked on a piece for a while, then meandered into the garden just outside. Soon, I was sipping and reading and meandering more than I was painting, so we bought an outside studio where discipline would embrace me more strongly than the pull to lounge or work in the garden for hours on end.

Becoming known for my distinct use of texture and color, a handful of new galleries beckoned. And as my presence grew, so grew my need for an agent who wasn't also running our business.

With The Black Iris thriving, Bill—who had been undeniably instrumental in launching my career—proposed expanding my opportunities for growth by opening our own gallery under his name. The idea of running two businesses was a bit overwhelming to me, but Bill had the head for it, and he also had a knack for finding the best people to run things when he wasn't around. So we opened the William Merrill Gallery, and Bill hired a skilled director named Glenn to run it. With Glenn's background in art and having pivotal connections, he also became my new manager as well as a dear friend.

In a nearly seamless transition, Glenn picked up where Bill left off, acquiring gallery showings for me across the US, in Canada, and in London, along with exhibitions in seven or eight museums.

Creating ten to twenty pieces per collection, I dabbled in various mediums and themes, always stretching myself artistically. While I definitely had my own style, I was never satisfied to stay with one motif for too long. If you envisioned my early career like pages of a book being turned, you would see abstracts, followed by expressions of movement, followed by old European doors, followed by thirty paintings of Mikhail Baryshnikov I created from photographs and memories of watching him dance live onstage. One even made the cover of *Orange County* magazine.

As my art gained more and more exposure, our home also landed on the radar for local journalists as a "house built for art." The *LA Times* and the *Orange County Register* featured gorgeous photographic spreads and personal interviews with us, and being music lovers who sat on the board of our local orchestra, our home became a hub for entertaining board members and musicians.

As my success escalated, I began mentoring other artists. I knew instinctively when someone had "the gift," and I drew on my background in teaching to help them bring that gift more boldly into the world. Watching my mentees score gallery exhibitions was like seeing my kindergartners' faces light up when they put letters on a page into words, or master simple equations, or even color inside the lines with a degree of pride. Achievement was achievement, no matter the scope. Every win was a stepping stone to the next, and it was deeply gratifying to witness those early milestones in people of all ages, each on their own particular path of personal evolution.

In some ways, in the current incarnation of myself, I felt unstoppable. I always believed there was no reason I couldn't achieve fame and notability as an artist. Other people made it big in their fields. Why not me? But I was also keenly aware of how fragile an art career was, that no artist—or actor, or musician, or writer—could ever take his success for granted. The arts were fickle; people could love you one day and lose interest the next. Perhaps from years of lack, I both relished the material possessions wealth afforded us and remained mindful that it could be fleeting. I consciously attracted abundance, but I also stayed firmly rooted in humility and gratitude.

I had no idea that in not more than a decade—in the midst of the accolades and convivial dinner parties and exhibitions where my art sometimes sold out in a single night—that mindset would be the foundation for sustaining me through the most terrifying, upending, and spiritually defining period of my life.

PART THREE

The Interpretation

CHAPTER TWENTY-EIGHT

2006

Bill and I were in Miami on vacation when I felt the burning.

It's unusual for men to get urinary tract infections, but that's what it felt like. So, believing an antibiotic would probably do the trick, we saw a local doctor. He prescribed me with amoxicillin but told me I should see my doctor when we returned home, that it shouldn't go unchecked in case it was something more.

My initial reaction was anger—we were with a group of lovely friends in South Beach, and being on antibiotics meant I couldn't drink. So much for cocktail-induced fun! So I didn't give it much thought other than how it tainted our trip to Florida.

When we got back, I made an appointment with a new doctor closer to home than my regular doctor in L.A. He ordered a complete blood panel, which included a PSA test for prostate cancer screening. He assured me it was a normal test for men around fifty, and that it was particularly important if a man had a family history of cancer. He also sent me off with another round of antibiotics.

At first, he said nothing about my PSA—prostate-specific antigen—levels. When the burning didn't go away, he ordered another round of antibiotics. Then another. I didn't realize it at the time, but all those antibiotics were killing my healthy gut flora, which is what fuels the immune system, so the drugs that were supposed to get rid of the infection were actually suppressing my ability to fight it.

Later, I would become more aware that we really do live in a "pill for every ill" society—and that most Western doctors are immersed in a pharmaceutical mindset, not a "what does the body need to heal itself?" mindset.

But at that time, I was in the vortex of the system, and all I wanted was for the burning to go away when I used the bathroom.

So this doctor ordered another blood panel. When it came back, he called and asked me to come in, which of course scared me right away. Bill came with me, as he did to every appointment, assuring me that no matter what, I was going to be okay.

The doctor didn't beat around the bush. "Paul," he said, "your test results indicate that it's best if I refer you to a urologist. Your PSA level has gradually gone up over the last six months, so a specialist is a good idea at this point."

I was silent. *Why hadn't he mentioned this sooner? Why did he flood me with antibiotics instead of sending me to a specialist a long time ago?*

After losing so many relatives to cancer, I had always carried an underlying fear that I would one day be diagnosed with it too. But it never occurred to me that this stubborn infection that ended up taking several rounds of antibiotics and months to clear up was anything but a major annoyance.

He placed his hand on my shoulder, seeming to read my mind. "It doesn't mean it's cancer. It's just a smart next step. Just to be sure."

I nodded. "Okay."

But it certainly seemed more menacing to me than he tried to make it sound.

Before I saw the urologist, my research began.

I learned that men with a PSA level between four and ten have about a one in four chance of having prostate cancer. If the PSA is higher than ten, the chance of having prostate cancer increases to over fifty percent.

I wasn't told my exact number, so I didn't know yet what I was up against, but I naturally wanted to know why my PSA could be elevated. So I started digging into articles and books for answers.

Factors That Might Elevate PSA Levels

An enlarged prostate
Older age
Inflammation of the prostate gland
Ejaculation
Riding a bicycle
Certain urologic procedures
Certain medicines

I hadn't ridden a bike for a while, had any procedures, or taken any medications, but I did feel some relief that there were reasons my levels could be higher than normal that *didn't* mean the C-word. The thing was, until I had further tests, I wouldn't know if mine was a fluke not worth worrying about or news I hoped to never receive.

———

The appointment with the urologist was an exercise in humiliation from the moment it began.

After very little discussion, the doctor snapped on his gloves as if readying himself for a magic show, then positioned me for a routine rectal exam—which was anything but "routine" for me—to feel for abnormalities of the gland. Then, having me remain in that position, he administered a numbing cream and performed a series of biopsies that involved extracting fifteen separate samplings of the two cores of my prostate with a needle. Besides the palpable awkwardness, the procedure felt like being stung repeatedly by an insect, or having a rubber band snapped against my insides.

When he finally finished, he told me I could sit up. The paper liner stuck to me as I rotated, and I made loud crinkling sounds maneuvering the gown back around me as he peeled off his gloves.

"Your prostate feels healthy," he said. "No enlargement or hard spots."

"That's good," I managed, finding it hard to look him in the eye now that he had just probed my most intimate body part.

"I'm fairly confident there's no cancer, but we'll have to wait ten days for the biopsy report to be sure." He walked over to a trashcan and stepped on the foot pedal. The metal lid slammed open with a clang and he tossed his gloves inside.

"I'm going to give you a prescription for antibiotics to protect you from possible infection from the procedure." He scribbled it out and handed it to me. "And don't worry. It's common to have blood in your urine and semen for a week."

I couldn't decide if that was reassuring or troubling as I held the white-coat endorsement of suppressing my immunity yet again.

"You can get dressed now," he said. "I'll be in touch." And with that, he disappeared out the door as if he had just stopped by for a casual drink and had another bar to stop at before going home.

I sat still for a moment, my level of vulnerability like a nude hitch-hiker's on a busy highway. I couldn't wait to put my clothes back on. But as I scooted off the table, I sensed that clothing would only serve as an illusion. I could pull on pants, cover my torso with a shirt, slip on shoes, but nothing could camouflage the feeling I had that I'd been completely turned inside-out.

As each day ticked by, I did my best to brush away the thought of a potentially negative outcome, coating the canvas of my worry in layers upon layers of paint. But when the paint had dried and I scraped and chiseled at it to create the desired texture, those suffocated feelings escaped from their encasement, glaring at me like a wound from which I'd just pulled off a bandage.

The truth was, I had secretly hoped our family cancer would skip a generation the way some diseases do—not that I would ever wish it on my nieces and nephews, but more that I hoped it would somehow die before reaching them. Now, as the fears peered at me from the waxy waves and edges of the manipulated canvas, I was faced with the possibility that it would not only skip but that it had already attacked.

I dipped one of my large brushes into lime green paint, entertaining the thought that re-covering all the exposed parts, like a mason filling in the missing bricks of a wall, could silence the disease forever.

And that's when the phone rang.

My heart immediately sped up when I saw the number. I stared at it for a moment, then closed my eyes and took a cleansing breath before answering.

"Hello?"

"Hello, Paul?" the person said. "It's Dr. Wagner."

A thin veneer of geniality coated the clinical tone of his ingrained medical training. I instantly sensed there was a crack in the glaze as my stomach tensed.

"Hi, Dr. Wagner."

"I have your test results," he said, pausing only briefly. "They did come back positive for prostate cancer."

I immediately felt my body freeze as if immobilized by an invisible force. All I remember after that was him saying it was in a very early stage, and that it was only a small amount in one core of one lobe. He prescribed "watchful waiting" and said I wouldn't need to do anything for a while. He also said that I would probably need to have follow-up biopsies every several months, but that he didn't think I would require any kind of treatment for at least five years.

Having minimal education on the disease, I felt relieved that it didn't sound critical. But if there was cancer in my body, I wanted to get rid of it—*now*. In my state of naïveté, I didn't comment at the time, but I did think it odd that leaving cancer to grow and possibly spread before it required treatment sounded unwise, if not criminal.

So I threw myself into reading books, perusing the Internet, and talking to other men who had chosen different routes for treatment. I also interviewed four specialists for second opinions. Bill, Noel, who was a nurse, and our friend Glenn, who was suffering from bone cancer, all came with me for each of the interviews to help me objectively weigh my options.

The man we were all most impressed with and who I chose for my care was a urologist/radiologist who recommended that I undergo surgery. He shared with me his father's long and painful battle with prostate cancer, and he thought I might be spared his suffering if I did surgery first.

"It will give you a second line of defense if the cancer returns," he said. "Meaning you could still do radiation."

My head was spinning. I didn't even know what that meant. I had read that surgery and radiation had the same rate of cure—and both threatened my sexuality. The risks of impotence, incontinence, and other undesirable side effects scared the shit out of me.

Ultimately, after doing more in-depth research on surgery (always a risk of dying under the knife), radiation (virtually painless but could damage other organs and tissue and create *more* cancer cells in the process), and even cryotherapy (freezing the prostate), I opted not to do any of them.

At the time, I wasn't knowledgeable about integrative therapies, and because prostate cancer is slow growing and doesn't pose a significant risk of metastasis, I decided to take a little more time to explore less injurious options.

Spending untold hours on the Internet, I discovered a relatively new, painless, non-surgical protocol called proton radiation therapy, which was the most precise and advanced form of radiation treatment available and had incredible cure rates. After talking to several people who had chosen the therapy, I decided it was the one I was most comfortable with. I could have the treatment, maintain my quality of life, and quickly resume my normal activities. Best of all, it wouldn't cause harm to surrounding healthy tissue or organs.

Though the side effects of the treatment were minimal— nausea, vomiting, headaches—I didn't believe they could be worse than my self-imposed emotional trauma. The mere idea of going through cancer treatment, after what I had seen my mother endure, was paralyzing. It's impossible to have no fear in that situation, no matter how optimistic you are. Depression, anger, disbelief—they all poke their sinister fingers repeatedly at your mind, taunting you, testing you.

I knew I might come out of it all okay, but I certainly wouldn't come out unchanged.

CHAPTER TWENTY-NINE

June, 2008

I was craving total escape before I began treatment, and our annual trip to the quaint Bohemian seaside village of Sitges, Spain, was the perfect remedy.

We and several friends vacationed for three weeks every summer in Sitges, a coastal basin southwest of Barcelona where mansions and charming apartments for the well-to-do overlook the golden Mediterranean beaches and bustling seafront promenade. Besides its myriad shops and cafés, it's known for its typical Spanish nightlife. Most bars and restaurants stay open until three a.m.; nightclubs don't close until dawn.

The beaches, with their turquoise waters that tease the vanilla sand, are a banquet of moving art, overflowing with beautiful people. The view from anywhere affords a constantly shifting mélange of men and women chatting with friends, laughing with an umbrella-ed drink in hand, or running and splashing into the ocean, the lively prints and vibrant colors of their scant swimwear tangoing with the waves. The atmosphere is light with carefreeness and an aura of inclusiveness. Everyone is either absorbed in their own recreation, reveling in people-watching, keeping a watchful eye out for someone to flirt with, or flaunting their hard-earned muscles or God-given beauty for all who care to look.

In short, it's a playground for the uninhibited, and a spectacle for the observant.

A few days into our trip, I was relaxing under the sun and admiring the landscape when I noticed a tall, lean, intensely ripped young man with a shaved head and multiple tattoos. He was stretching and rubbing various parts of his glistening body with suntan lotion, flexing each muscle as if starring in a soft-porn flick. He seemed supremely confident and unaware that more and more people were becoming captivated with him as he performed his sexy self-massage. I found myself unable to take my eyes off him, partly because he was an Adonis, partly because he was quite a showman, and partly because his tattoos grabbed my attention.

At the time, I was in the process of researching and developing a new series of paintings centered on different genres of tattoos. My criteria in choosing subjects to interview and then paint was that I had to be physically and intellectually attracted to them, and their tattoos had to tell some kind of story.

The symbolism behind tattoos and why people chose them fascinated me. I couldn't see this man's closely from where I was sitting, but his chiseled features were hard not to admire. Throughout the day, we locked eyes on each other and exchanged a friendly smile. Then, as the sun began to set, our group of eight took off to have a cocktail and walk down the main street before dinner.

Strolling and making small talk, I felt a magnetic pull to look to the right. When I did, I saw the man from the beach sitting on a ledge with a male friend. His stunning blue eyes met mine for a few seconds and I felt an electric charge go through my body. Bill and our friends teased me a bit about the encounter, and then we made our way back to the hotel to clean up and get dressed for dinner.

In Spain, dinner is served between eight and ten; everyone takes a siesta beforehand, and nighttime meals can often last until midnight. After that, it's off to the bars or nightclubs where people party together until sunrise.

After a delicious meal and several carafes of sangria, we ambled down a narrow cobblestone alley where numerous dance and other clubs—gay, straight, and blended—beckoned us. We would peek our heads in to see if we liked the vibe, then saunter to the next to see if we liked that one better. Deciding to pop in to a men's bar and survey it for the gang, I had started down the steps to the entrance when I felt a tug on my tank top, then someone grabbed my arm.

"Hey, bud," I heard with an Irish-sounding accent.

I turned. And there he was again.

"What's your name?" he asked.

"Paul." I tipped my head back slightly. "And you?"

"I'm Dylan. And this is Ian." He threw a thumb Ian's way and they both smiled.

Suddenly, I was rendered speechless as if I were a preteen boy being asked to dance for the first time, with three hundred classmates watching.

Dylan's bright blue eyes drew me almost hypnotically, and his body was like a pristine sculpture. Except for the body art, he almost didn't seem real. I immediately glanced away as my heart stepped up its pace. Instead of acknowledging him, I moved hastily into the club. When I didn't come back out right away, Bill and our friends followed me inside.

We all ordered drinks, and I purposely engaged myself in deep conversation with one of our friends in case Dylan came into the bar. I wanted to be certain I looked completely unavailable. Just experiencing the feelings Dylan ignited in me made me feel like I was cheating on Bill.

As the night progressed, we all decided to find another dive bar where we could dance. A short walk later, we entered a lively club and ordered another round of drinks. A large group of people were chatting and laughing while they grooved to a disco song and we joined them. I was caught up in the rhythm of the music and the booze swirling through my body when a towering, rugged-looking man approached me and leaned toward my ear.

"I'm a friend and bodyguard for a guy who wants to meet you," he said. "He's on the second floor."

I pulled back and laughed. I thought one of my friends was pulling a prank on me.

The guy leaned in again. "My friend is a high-profile athlete, and he wants to meet you upstairs alone."

I nodded with a cavalier sigh. "Oh really? Well, tell your friend that I'm a famous, international high-profile artist and that I'm here with my many bodyguards, and that if he wants to meet me, he'll have to come down and meet us all."

My friends howled with laughter as the guy walked away.

About ten minutes later, the bodyguard returned with a serious look on his face.

"My friend really wants to meet you one on one," he said. "He says your group is too large and intimidating."

It sounded hokey but I thought, *What the hell?* The charade intrigued me and the flattery of being found attractive more than once that night got the better of me.

So I eased away from my group and went upstairs to find out who the mystery man was.

He was sitting in the dark, illuminated only by a strobe and a few dim lights behind the bar.

"Dylan?" I said, squinting and walking toward him. "You're the one who wanted to meet me? What's up with all the pomp and circumstance?"

He looked confused.

"The bodyguard?"

"Oh," he said nodding. Then he added with his heavy accent, "Sorry to be such a pain, bud, but I'm an athlete."

He began explaining how he was a rugby star in the UK, who he played for, and so on. I admitted I didn't follow the sport in the US, so he gave me a quick schooling on Rugby 101. Not being a sports fan, I couldn't have cared less. But the way his syllables danced in what I learned was a Welsh accent, coupled with his commanding presence, had me in a trance. I forgot I was bored as I listened intently to the details of his sport and the country he loved so much.

When the conversation pivoted to me, I shared about being an artist and that I was from Southern California. He seemed fascinated by my life and my art, and he was particularly interested in the new series I was working on. As his eyes followed my lips while I spoke, we seemed to be in a world all our own.

Before I knew it, an hour had passed, and I told him I needed to get back to Bill and our friends.

"I'd love to learn more about you and your tattoos," I said in parting. "And maybe you could come to the exhibition in America next year."

As I walked away, he said, "How about meeting me a bit later by yourself? For a drink?"

It was already past 3:00. Dawn would be breaking soon. "I don't know," I said, shaking my head. "I'm with my partner and we're staying in an apartment on the main beach."

He sat staring at me with those hypnotic eyes. Being pretty intoxicated, I was fair game. "I guess I could try to meet up with you," I conceded.

He told me where and when to meet him, and I hustled downstairs to rejoin my group. Bill gave me a look that told me he was put off by how long I was gone, but not wanting to seem jealous in front of our friends, he said nothing.

"So who was the mystery man?" someone asked.

"Yeah, details, details," someone else chimed, elbowing me.

Feeling like I was on the witness stand, I spilled who Dylan was, his rugby career, and how flattered I was that this rugged and handsome young man showed interest in me. Bill played along, but I could tell he wondered where my head was.

We staggered back to the apartment, and our friends Bennett and Glenn threw themselves onto the couch. Bill fixed us all nightcaps, and we sat around reflecting on the night we'd just had. But the conversation quickly morphed into background noise as I sat conspiring how to clandestinely meet Dylan.

As I was masterminding my plan, a loud voice crowded my thoughts.

This isn't like you, Paul. You and Bill are solid. You have a rule that everything between you is transparent. No secrets. Never infidelity. What are you doing trying to sneak away and see this guy?

Feeling restless, and with the crazy amount of booze I'd consumed giving me gumption, I nonchalantly announced that I was going to slip out for a bit to chat with Dylan about using him as a model.

Bill looked at me as if I'd just lost my mind. Bennett and Glenn had the same bewildered look. They each gave me rational reasons for why it was a bad idea, but I was determined to leave.

"If you walk out this door," Bill said, "you won't come back through it as you know it."

In a fit of irrational rage that no one had ever seen in me before, I lashed out at Bill. "Oh really? Is that how it's going to be? Well, too bad. I won't be controlled by anyone. *Ever.* Especially not *you!*"

My harsh words started an argument of epic proportions that our friends tried desperately to mediate, but to no avail. As each unwarranted slam flew out of my mouth, I knew I would regret it. But in that moment, I didn't care. Something had completely taken me over, and the alcohol didn't help.

Suddenly, my rage escalated to a point of violence. I had never hit Bill before, and even in my unreasonable state, I knew I didn't want to start now. So I hastened to the wall and punched my fist into it with all the force I had. I instantly screamed and buckled to the floor as I felt the splintering of the tiny bones in my hand and the immediate throbbing pain.

Glenn and Bennett appeared quickly with an ice pack, and Bill said we should go to the hospital. I knew instinctively that I was badly injured and would probably need surgery, but I wasn't willing to end our vacation for it. I also wasn't willing to give up my chance of meeting up with Dylan to discuss including him in my series.

So I refused to get medical help, even as I watched my hand swell to twice its size. I insisted that I'd manage with pain pills and ice, so Bill, who had completely had it with me at that point, got me some meds from an all-night pharmacy where they didn't require a prescription.

———

Late that morning, we met up with our friends on the beach. Someone placed a Bloody Mary in my left hand.

"Ouch," he said, pointing to the right.

I just shook my head.

Lounging on chaises, we exchanged stories about the night before. I explained away my swollen, bandaged hand as a bad fall I took on the way back to the apartment, that I had tripped and landed full force on a rock. Everyone believed me except our friend Joost, who was a physician in Holland. He took one look at my hand and rolled his eyes.

"Head to the hospital immediately," he said, seeing through the lie. "This was no 'trip and fall' injury."

But stubborn as a red-wine stain on white carpet, I waved off his advice and endured the pain.

The rest of our trip, I was hopped up on pain pills. Each time they began to wear off, my hand throbbed so excruciatingly with every beat of my heart that I wished I could be knocked out.

Except for the time I maneuvered to spend with Dylan.

Drawn by some inexplicable force, I became obsessed with interviewing and photographing Dylan for the series. I pled my case with Bill that I couldn't pass up the opportunity to include such an ideal model in my new collection, but I also couldn't deny that I was flattered by the interest Dylan showed in me.

His plentiful tattoos were an array of symbols—birds, praying hands, stars, geometric shapes, a scorpion, a Celtic cross. I wanted to hear the story behind the choice of each one, and Dylan was more than willing to share. Dragging out our time together, he would outline each tattoo with his finger as he explained its significance, and I would watch the air become streaked with the fiery hues of his sensuality.

Without articulating it, his tone and body language made it clear that he was attracted to me. But I had never been unfaithful to Bill, and it wasn't in my character to cave to a physical affair. Yet, there I was, probably giving some unintended sign to this man that I was attracted to him as well, but like a coy schoolgirl, had no intention of consummating it. Intense guilt chased me the entire race, but somehow, the security that was Bill's and my relationship gave me the false sense that I could pursue this temporary infatuation without consequence.

I couldn't have been more wrong.

CHAPTER THIRTY

T he day after we returned home from Spain, I managed to get a last-minute appointment with my doctor. Sitting in his office, I gave him the same story I had given my friends—that I had fractured my hand by falling onto a rock. I could tell he didn't buy it, and when he slapped the X-rays onto the wall, it confirmed his suspicion—that the only way the bones could be fractured the way they were was from a boxer's punch.

"So what'd ya hit?" he asked me. "Some jerk?"

Embarrassed to own the real reason, I shook my head. "No, I really did fall."

He pulled back. The bullshit meter on his face was at full bar. "Come on, Paul. I know a boxer's punch when I see it. What'd ya hit?"

I hated to admit the truth, but I knew my game was up. "Oh all right. I punched a wall."

He nodded as if he'd played witness to this scenario a hundred times.

"Well," he said, a bit arrogantly, rolling his stool toward me, then emitting that "puff" sound as he landed on the vinyl seat, "if you don't want your hand to become arthritic and curl up weird, you're going to need surgery."

He pulled his lips inward as five horizontal lines grew deeper in his forehead.

I glanced away. I knew he wasn't going to take no for an answer, but a no is what I gave him anyway.

"Paul, you're not only messing with your mobility here, you're messing with your art career."

I looked him in the eye. "I know that."

"So you're willing to just throw that away because you don't want to have surgery?"

I shrugged slightly. "I'm just not sure it's what I should do."

But it wasn't just that I was indecisive about having surgery. It was a voice telling me to get a second opinion.

So I consulted with our dear friend, Benoit, who lived in France and had been on our Sitges trip. He possessed a deep spiritual connection that allowed him to see and feel things from the divine, and I asked him to "tune in" to my situation by phone. When he did, he said he felt strongly that I should not have the surgery; if I did, I'd never paint the same again.

Shortly after we spoke, he traveled to the States and gave me a session in person. He asked me to lie on the floor, and then he went into a trance. As he channeled the divine, I recall being overcome by emotion. Then, for thirty minutes to an hour, my arms, as if their own entities out of my control, levitated over my head. While I didn't completely understand what had happened during the session, when Benoit came out of the trance, he told me he felt certain about his declaration that I should not have the surgery.

He also told me to stay completely away from Dylan, that the unrest he sensed coming from my body wasn't solely related to my injury.

Despite most everyone thinking I was nuts, I took Benoit's advice and declined the surgery. My instinct told me he was right, even if my doctor disagreed. Plus I was due to start my proton therapy, which surgery would have delayed. All in all, I believed I was doing the right thing.

I only wish I'd taken his advice about Dylan.

————

When I showed up at my preparatory appointment for the proton therapy with a soft cast on my hand, I incited the telltale grimaces that a child might get falling in the mud before church on Easter Sunday.

Before I left for Spain, the doctors made a fiberglass cast of my body, and I was warned not to gain more than two pounds or I wouldn't fit properly in it for the treatment. Precision is key to this therapy in order to target the cancer—and only the cancer—cells, so I had to be especially careful about what I ate. They hadn't warned me not to get injured.

If the cast exceeded the weight limit, or I couldn't navigate my arm such that it didn't impede the procedure, I'd have to have a whole new body cast made—at a high price tag out of pocket—which would delay the entire process even more. Unfortunately, I wouldn't know for sure until the first day of treatment if my tirade in Spain would have even more unpleasant consequences than I was already facing.

So until then, the doctor once again walked me through what to expect in the procedure. Though I already knew the details from my introductory appointment and all I had read, the actuality of the humiliating position I'd be in for the first time the following week, and for fifty-three weekdays after that, was sobering. But I was mentally and physically committed to making it work, despite the embarrassment. I knew in my heart it was my best shot.

For two and a half months, I would make a two-and-a-half-hour drive each weekday from Laguna Beach to the treatment center in Loma Linda. Preparation for the therapy itself would take an hour, but before that, I'd have to sit in the waiting room until I was called into the gantry, which is what they call the holding tank where people await availability of the treatment room. There would be three gantries designated for prostate cancer; treatment times would be randomly assigned day to day from 7:00 a.m. to 11:00 p.m., but even after being given a time slot, the wait once called to a gantry could be up to eight hours.

After changing into a backless gown with nothing on underneath, I would lie in a corridor until my turn came up. Once inside the radiation room, they would carefully situate me in the fiberglass cast where I'd have to lie still for fifteen minutes, in a position akin to giving birth. But before that timer started ticking, they would have to prep me for the actual radiation. This would entail a tech inserting a nine-inch tube with a deflated balloon attached to the end into my anal cavity. He or she would then irrigate the tube to inflate the balloon with water. This would move the organs near my prostate out of the way, so that no radiation reached anything but the prostate. It would take some time to make sure the balloon was in its proper place before the proton therapy could be administered.

When the fifteen minutes were up, it would all happen in reverse, and I'd make the two-and-a-half-hour drive back home to Laguna.

Exhausting, to say the least.

But it was better than surgery. Supremely better than chemo. Certainly better than traditional radiation.

I was willing to do whatever it took to get rid of that sonofabitch way before five years went by and it was too late to do much more than pray for a miracle.

CHAPTER THIRTY-ONE

Proton Therapy

DAY 1

Men can put on the brave face society has imposed on them, but waiting with dozens of other men—all in various stages of illness—for cancer treatment, there's not a man in that room who isn't working overtime, if not subconsciously, to suppress his fear.

You wonder, despite it being awkward, if you should strike up casual conversation with the guy sitting next to you. Sometimes he takes the leap first. He may ask what stage you're in, how many treatments you've had. You answer and he nods. You ask the same of him. He answers, you nod. But in general, most just try to look anywhere but at the other men in the room. Staring is rude. Glances are uncomfortable. When you catch someone's eye, do you smile politely? *Is that appropriate in this circumstance?* So most read to pass the time, or occupy themselves on their phones, or work on their laptops. Sometimes you'll see an older man—one who might carry an old flip phone for emergencies only—gazing expressionless at the floor after he's finished reading the newspaper, cloaked in his generational stoicism, with no hand-held technology to distract his thoughts. Some make friends with each other after sharing the waiting room day after day, and the lucky men like me who have a friend or loved one with them can engage in familial chatter on and off. But no matter how you fill the hours, time stretches out before you like the yellow brick road to Oz, with that same hope that what's at the end is what will cure you, and that same not knowing if when you came to a fork in the road, you indeed chose the right path.

———

That first day, Bill and I arrive early. I don't recall how long it takes before they call my name to enter the gantry; all I remember is that it takes hours, and that as soon as I hear my name, my eyes well with tears.

A nurse escorts me down the long hallway to the radiation dressing room where I change into the backless garment. I instinctively pull the two seams as close together as they'll go, but there's still a revealing gap. I lie down with other men surrounding me and wait.

Sometime later, I'm called into the therapy room. Besides a nurse, there are two techs and my doctor, as well as several other assistants assigned to monitors.

I'm guided to step onto a platform where the team will help situate me in my body mold. Because my soft cast is a potential issue, everyone seems extra anxious. As I begin climbing into the mold, I'm overly cautious of my hand and I lose my balance. My gown slips to the floor. I stand there naked, frozen. Multiple pairs of eyes just stare. Beads of sweat form on my forehead and my hand trembles as I awkwardly bend down to pull the gown back up.

It takes some navigating to get me into the body mold with my cast, but I'm relieved when we finally do. The intense focus on my wrist and hand has momentarily eclipsed my embarrassment of having to put my feet up into stirrups with my private parts fully exposed.

Once settled, I'm told they're going to start the procedure. I shudder slightly as I feel someone gently smear lubricant on me. Then, I feel the person begin to insert the tube with the balloon into my rectum. But because I'm nervous and tense, the tech has a hard time. The probe keeps cutting into the wall of my anus.

"Just try to relax," the technician says calmly.

"Relax?" I practically yell. "You lie here naked in a room full of strangers and let me put a tube up your ass, then see if you can relax."

The room quiets.

After several attempts, the probe is in place and I feel the water filling up the balloon. When it's full and they've verified that my other organs are out of harm's way, they remind me not to move, not even a little.

I hear a hum as the radiation is administered.

It is the longest fifteen minutes of my life.

Fifty-three more to go.

CHAPTER THIRTY-TWO

Proton Therapy

DAY 2

My stomach is gurgling and I'm spitting up acid. It tastes awful and I dread when it happens.

But it's not from the treatment. It's from nerves.

It actually started a few weeks ago. That's how I know it's not the proton therapy that's causing it.

The more likely reason is that Dylan has become my muse in a way that may be innocent to me, but I can tell it's not to him. Maybe it's not to me either. Maybe I'm treading on delicate ground, being led on a leash by my fragile ego.

I realize that the best way for me to endure each treatment is to detach mentally once I'm in the body mold. Modesty is out the window. Nerves only make staying still more difficult. I have to remember that people all over the world have it worse—sometimes day in and day out, for years on end. If they can endure, I can do this one thing for fifty-three more days.

A lot of people with cancer don't even know this is an option for them. I'm one of the lucky ones. I have the means to afford it. I don't even have to worry about taking time off from a job. It's a long drive, but it could be a lot farther away, in another state even.

I'm one of the lucky ones.

"Ready, Paul?" I hear.

I offer a muffled "Mm hm," close my eyes, and it begins . . .

Dylan. I can't stop thinking about him. I don't know why I'm so drawn to him, but I can't wait to paint him from the pictures I took in Spain. He has made me feel even more excited about this series. He's got charisma, that's for sure. The sort of reckless kind that Dan had, not the classy kind that Bill has.

Dan.

What a roller coaster that was.

He was the love of my young life, but damn . . . what a hot and cold and dysfunctional time. I couldn't help the love I felt for him, though. But of course when we broke up, what did I feel? Abandoned. I always feel fucking abandoned. I can't even bear it when my friends leave a restaurant before I do, or God forbid a hotel or a group vacation. It should be no big deal but for me, I feel ABANDONED when they leave. That's why I always have to leave first. I just can't handle that feeling of being left.

So yeah, it makes sense what happened after Dan. Sex became linked with abandonment. Once that happened, the link was like a chain I couldn't break. Dan and I had great sex. Then he left me. Or I left him. Either way, it didn't last. Something just turned off in me. I guess maybe I thought if I let myself get sexually involved with another man I loved, he would leave me too. But if I held back somehow, maybe I could control the relationship working. It's like my mind was telling my body not to let go, not to feel too much ecstasy or pleasure. Then I wouldn't have to relate sex to the feeling of abandonment.

I feel so sad thinking about it. But it makes sense. It's like those experiments they've done with people where they have them eat a certain food while they watch something disturbing. Then the food gets linked with a bad feeling and the person doesn't want that food anymore. Or some song reminds you of a sad time in your life, so every time it plays, you rush to turn it off so you can turn the sad feeling off with it. Or someone hurt you when you were wearing certain clothes, and you can never wear those clothes again so you get rid of them.

The feelings are all connected with tangible things. For some people, it's food or songs or clothes . . . but for me it had to be sex. What a rip-off. I was created to enjoy sex, not be afraid of it. But that's what happened to me. I became afraid of what it could mean. And then everyone assumes all gay men are promiscuous and thoughtless about sex. But that's a completely unfair assumption. Yeah, a LOT of men have perpetuated that *belief by acting that way, but so have lots of straight men and women. I think we all have baggage we haul around. Some people give themselves to strangers without a thought because of hurt they carry. And some can barely give themselves to the soul mates they'll love till the end of time . . .*

CHAPTER THIRTY-THREE

Proton Therapy

DAY 8

've adopted a song as my mantra called "Pocket Full of Sunshine" by British artist Natasha Bedingfield. I crank the car stereo and play it over and over on our drive to Loma Linda.

> *Take me away, a secret place*
> *A sweet escape, take me away . . .*

The song says that the sun is on my side, that in the darkness, there's light. It says that when I smile up to the sky, I know I'll be all right . . .

"Ready, Paul?"
"Mm hm," I answer . . .

I have to stop thinking about Dylan. But the more he reaches out to me, the more I want him to. I keep asking him to share more of his life story with me so that I can get to know his true self. The more I know him, the better I can create incredible paintings of him. But I know that being in touch with him like this is pushing it. I know I'm not his therapist, but I think I've become that for him. And the more he shares, the more I want to be there for him because I know he's struggling and I want to help. I don't lead him on in any way. I stay pretty objective. But I guess it gives me an ego boost to be someone's confidant I never expected.

I guess there's a part of me that needs that.

I wonder why?

Am I still dying inside to feel special because Marge and Ray tried so hard to destroy that feeling in me?

God, just the thought of them makes me sick. I'm so glad I hardly ever think of them. What a couple of monsters. They must have had some serious pain inside that they could both be so cruel to children. How could they not realize how scary that time was for us? It's like in old movies . . . they always depict the orphans like trash. They're pushed around and abused and made to feel like being an orphan is a disease, like it's their fault their parents died or left them. That's how Marge and Ray made us feel. Like something was wrong with us. That we deserved to be treated badly because our parents were going through a tough time. I just don't understand what lives inside people that makes them feel entitled to hurt children like that. How can some adults lack compassion for little kids? It doesn't make sense to me.

Like Mrs. Secker. She was another one. A total double whammy living with Marge and Ray and having Mrs. Secker for my first real teacher. It's no wonder I had issues. That mean-ass woman had a class full of kindergartners who were scared and nervous and just starting out in school. She had the chance to make it wonderful, but instead she was mean. All she knew how to do was lay down rules and talk to us in her stern voice. I can still hear it. She was so sure she had to be that way to keep us all in line. I don't think it ever occurred to her to just be kind and empathetic. Wasn't she ever a scared little girl?

God, and then there was that obnoxious bus driver. Shouting rules into that fucking megaphone. Warning us all the time. She drove me crazy too. I know some of the kids were unruly, but Gail and I weren't. We were so good . . .

We did all the chores in that twisted house. We ate the inferior food and were never allowed to complain. They could have at least tried to make a temporary family for us. But they didn't. It was a long time ago, and maybe I shouldn't care now, but it still makes me sad that they thought treating us the way they did was okay. We were at our most vulnerable. That age when everything imprints you for the rest of your life. And what did they do? They made us feel unloved and unwanted . . .

I can still see myself as that sad little boy.

I want to say:

"You are special and beautiful. There is something missing in them,

not in you. I know it's hard to understand at your age, but trust me when I tell you that you didn't do anything wrong. Mom and Dad's problems aren't because of you. They're dealing with adult things that have nothing to do with you or anything you've done. This is just a temporary stop. I know it feels like forever, and I know they treat you rotten here, but just know that it won't last . . ."

CHAPTER THIRTY-FOUR

Proton Therapy

DAY 15

Bill and I came today only to wait for hours and then be told that the machine is down. It happens sometimes, they say. In a way it's a reprieve, but mostly it's annoying, inconvenient, and prolonging this even more.

We crank my mantra song on the way home, and I let my voice be one with Natasha's.

> *Take me away to better days*
> *Take me away to a hiding place . . .*

CHAPTER THIRTY-FIVE

Proton Therapy

DAY 22

The machine is working today, but that could change. Once you drive two and a half hours to be told the machine is down, you can't help but wonder if you'll drive all that way and have to turn around and go home. It's like when a parent picks you up from school on time week after week, and you count on it because you know you can. And then one day, your mother's late. She has a good reason, but still. Every day after that, you wonder if she'll be late again . . .

It's a delicate thing to count on someone. Especially when you love them so much. You always want to believe in them, even when they let you down. But it's hard when you're a child and the person is your mother . . .

I was so scared after we left the Fletchers and moved into the beach house that we'd have to go back into foster care again. If Mom got sick. If we didn't behave. If Mom and Dad fought. It was a horrible feeling to carry around. Nothing was certain, even when it felt like it should be. Once you're abandoned like that, it never really goes away.

Then it happened again. No one really knows the story because I don't tell anyone. It's just too painful. I begged so hard and cried so hard. But Mom wouldn't give in. All because her Al-Anon sponsor had a nice house, and she always wanted a son. Mom actually thought I'd have a better life with this woman. I'd have my own room instead of sharing a bed with her and my sisters. She thought I'd like working in their little restaurant so I'd have some money for myself. So she sent me off to live with her. Didn't she realize that changing schools in the ninth grade was the worst possible age to leave my friends? I was completely destroyed.

But she thought she was doing me a huge favor. All I could think of was that she didn't want me all over again.

I felt like a total pariah in that school. I failed every course and got treated like an outsider. It was kind of fun working in the diner, but the main thing I remember was being miserable for four straight months. I kept begging Mom to let me come home, and she kept saying no. I couldn't understand it. She was the one who seemed to love me more than anyone on earth, but she sent me away again.

It still hurts thinking about that time. I was in so much pain the whole time I was away. I know now that she really thought she was doing something wonderful for me because she loved me so much. She thought I was stuck in our house like the odd guy out with all those females. And maybe I was. But then I lived in that big beautiful house with my own phone and TV in my room and all I could think of was how I missed our tiny apartment in Broadway Village. I still wanted to have nice things and a big house on the ocean one day, but I did miss my family. I missed my mother's love more than anything. I guess I even missed arguing with my sisters and sleeping in the same bed with them because it's what I was used to. I didn't realize at the time how significant that was. All I knew was that I wanted to come home more than I wanted my own bedroom . . . or having my own paycheck . . . or the cool things that well-meaning woman bought me to give me what she thought would make a boy my age happy . . .

CHAPTER THIRTY-SIX

Proton Therapy

DAY 31

The machine's been down twice in the last week. It feels like the damn thing is mocking me when that happens. I guess it's all part of helping me learn to go with the flow . . .

This is fucking uncomfortable. There's no denying it. The balloon thing feels weird. I'm embarrassed to be naked in front of these people. Seeing them every day doesn't make me feel more comfortable with them.

Think of something else. Try to go with the flow.

Fuck the flow!

Think of something else . . .

Okay, okay . . . that article I read in the waiting room. It talked about being aware of red flags in relationships. That makes me think of Dan. Were there red flags? It's hard to say. I have to put the later years aside and really think. Were there signs that he wasn't good for me early on?

He did more drugs than I did and drank too much. I didn't like that but I couldn't stop him. I guess I could have seen that both were addictions that would get more intense for him. But I didn't know that for sure. It wasn't worth leaving him over at the time.

So when did it start to change?

Well, he started cheating on me. That was a red flag for sure. It wasn't a one-time thing we cried over and made up after. He kept doing it, even though we fought about it.

Fighting. That's a red flag. Couples shouldn't fight more than they get along. They shouldn't try to beat the shit out of each other when they get mad either. But the make-up sex. That's why it seemed okay. The make-up sex made everything seem okay . . . at least until the next fight.

But then Dan wouldn't clean up his act for me. Another red flag. I guess he thought the nice apartment and clothes and the lifestyle he provided me gave him freedom to do some shitty things. He didn't understand that it doesn't work that way. Hell, I didn't understand it doesn't work that way.

But I did, though. I felt it was off balance in a big way. It was kind of a slow slide, but then yeah, I knew from that sinking feeling I'd have more and more.

So why did I stay? Why was I so attached to someone who wasn't good for me? Where was my backbone?

. . .

Oh my God . . . why didn't I ever see it before?

That's exactly what Mom did with Dad.

She fell hard for him and his charm, like I did with Dan. Their love life was magnetic, just like mine and Dan's. She put up with a lot of his crap because she loved him. Another ditto.

So I guess I became my own mother.

Holy shit, I did. I only had my parents as role models, and I watched my mother do the same thing. Then I subconsciously mimicked her.

Wow. Maybe Mom, Dan, and I were more alike than I ever realized. Maybe that's why we were so close. We all loved each other, but I think we each made some of the destructive choices we did because we didn't really know how to love ourselves . . .

CHAPTER THIRTY-SEVEN

Proton Therapy

DAY 32

It's become more routine, I'll say that. But it's still as uncomfortable and embarrassing as hell to have this procedure. I keep reminding myself that it's giving me an excellent chance of never having to face cancer again, that I just have to hang in there for a couple more weeks and it will all be over.

All I know is, I'm over halfway there, and I've gotten pretty good at living solely in reflection the moment the machine starts to hum. I've also started saying affirmations, which give me a lot of strength . . .

I am strong. I am healed. I am a warrior . . .

Yesterday. That was a pretty intense aha moment.

Leave it to me, the boy who adored his mother, to actually become her in ways usually a daughter would.

It's kinda funny actually. Except that it's sad too. It's sad that neither one of us felt enough self-respect to leave a bad relationship before it got so ugly that we finally cracked.

I can see now how easy it is to judge someone for certain things they do in relationships when you don't have the whole story. We don't know what kind of imprint has been stamped on a person from their families or their DNA. We don't know why some people only learn from making the worst kinds of mistakes.

I know I should have left Dan sooner. It would have been smarter and healthier to do that. But I also have to give myself a break. I was young. He was my first love, my first sexual experience. He was the first person I was able to just be me with (besides Lynda), and he was hot! So of course when we fell in love, I was happier than ever. I could finally express myself as a full human being.

Now, I'm here lying in this thing at age fifty-four, trying to save my health. It seems ridiculous to regret what I did or didn't do in my late teens and twenties. What good does that do now? I know I could have saved myself some painful years and consequences if I'd made different decisions. But I probably had to go through those rough patches to learn what I didn't want to happen in a relationship the next time. Bill is certainly nothing like Dan (except for having piercing blue eyes and being gorgeous!), and look at us . . . we've been together almost thirty years. I love how blown away people are when we tell them that.

But Dan will always be a part of me. He really did help define the young me, in good ways and bad. I know he was toxic to me, but I learned from it. I found out the hard way that no one should settle for a dysfunctional relationship. My parents did and look what happened. Mom went through so much pain over Dad.

But I'll always be grateful to Dan too. He really did take care of me, at least in material ways. He was an addict and a player, but he was also generous and nurturing.

And he never did stop loving me. He was still trying to get me back even after Bill and I got together. He was so damn confident in himself. The guy shows up wanting a job at the shop, and Bill hires him. But that's Bill. He doesn't act jealous or weird . . . he sees that Dan has real talent as a designer and welcomes him into our lives as a friend. Some people thought it was weird, but not Bill . . . he's not insecure like most people in that situation. We all hung out together and Bill was a real class act, just like always.

Yeah. I probably ignored some red flags when I was young and in love. But it must say something good about me that I got it right the second time around . . .

CHAPTER THIRTY-EIGHT

Proton Therapy

DAY 45

The machine was down again yesterday. I'm trying to stay positive in all this, but God, I hate making that drive for nothing.

The good news is they say there's shrinkage of the tumor, though I don't know how they can tell when the mass was supposedly minuscule to begin with. What I do know is that I'm becoming stronger than I ever thought I could be. I feel my healing happening and believe that it is. The support around me is off the charts, and I feel increasingly empowered the more I read and follow the sage guidance of inspiring spiritual teachers.

I've also learned to breathe, just breathe . . .

I am strong. I am healed. I am a warrior . . .

I'm on the swings. There is nothing I love more than this feeling of the sun on my back and the air flowing over my face. Up and back. Up and back. I pump my legs so I can fly higher and higher into the sky. I'm at school. The kids are counting to one hundred and it's annoying. Now I'm in a park where I used to go on weekends sometimes. Just to be on the swings with no time limit. I close my eyes and remember how I always dreamed of a better life. Of living in a beautiful house. Of having a yard to play in. I don't want to stop swinging but the adult me wants to run alongside little me and tell him to slow down. I want him to get off the swing, just for a minute, so I can hug him. "You'll have these things," I tell my young self. "I know you can't see it. But you will, I promise." I've never hugged my young self before. The emotion I feel is intense. He's so vulnerable and sensitive. "Your sensitivity is a good thing," I say. "Don't let anyone tell you it's not." I see that little face looking at me, and I cry. I hug him tightly to me. We're both crying. I stroke his hair with the palm of my hand. I'm aware of how big my other arm feels around his tiny body. I know how insecure he feels and it breaks my heart. I see the rough road ahead for him. Instinctively, I want to protect him from the pain he'll face, but I instantly know it's all part of his path. "Hang in there, sweetheart," I say. "Don't stop dreaming. I know you can't see it now, but your dreams really will come true."

I see so much promise in little me. He's been born during a time when it won't be easy to be himself. Society will make him feel like he has no choice but to lie, hide, pretend. And he will. I want to tell him that as he gets older, it won't matter as much what people think. And who are they anyway to judge him? Why is their way the only way? What right do they have to say that he wasn't created in God's image exactly how he's supposed to be? He can't change how he feels inside about men any more than another man could suddenly not be attracted to women because someone told him he shouldn't be. It doesn't work like that. But they will still try to convince him something's wrong with him.

If only I could assure that sweet, innocent little boy that he's exactly who he's supposed to be . . .

CHAPTER THIRTY-NINE

Proton Therapy

DAY 50

I'm on the final leg, my last week of putting myself at the mercy of doctors and technicians to obliterate this tiny demon that took residence in my body. It's an indescribable relief to know I only have five more of these before it's over.

I won't even entertain the possibility that this won't work. There's no way I've put myself through all these demeaning treatments for nothing. The time. The money. The worry.

There's no way I've gone through this just to learn to tune into the divine whispers of what my life has been striving to teach my soul.

Or have I?

I am strong. I am healed. I am a warrior . . .

Now that I think about it, it's no wonder I have prostate cancer. Maybe people get cancer in the place where they have some kind of emotional toxic buildup. Mom couldn't take care of her family the way she wanted to and look at her. She got breast cancer . . .

And all of her sisters . . . they had mothering deficiencies too, and every one of them died of breast or ovarian cancer. The two mothers of all mothering body parts.

It really does make sense . . .

I knew I was gay when I was four, but I couldn't express it. Dad wasn't the best role model. Then Grandpa messed up my view of sexuality when I was just a kid. I can hear some people now. "See . . . that's why he's gay." But you can't make a person gay. I wish people would finally get that once and for all. YOU CANNOT MAKE A PERSON GAY. AND YOU CANNOT FORCE SOMEONE TO BE STRAIGHT EITHER. It's a lie and a tragedy to say you can. People are just people, for God's sake. And why do people feel such a need to label everyone? Kinsey totally figured out that people love and are attracted to others on a scale. It's not just gay or straight and it doesn't need to be. I happened to know when I was four that I was drawn to men. Nothing made me gay. It's just the way I was born. People have tried so hard to make it something ugly and wrong, but it's not. It was confusing, though, I'll say that.

I get molested in high school by the football star . . . the older art professors want to sleep with me. I can't be my true self for years and years. And then Dan and I break up and sex equals abandonment for me. I've never been completely comfortable with intimacy since. Not such a big surprise that a disease forms in that area of my body. Where you hold pain and shame, it builds up into dis-ease.

And now I'm here, with a group of strangers looking at me with a tube up my ass. They're probably assuming that it's not such a foreign thing, that all gay men are into anal sex so it's something we're used to. The irony is that I've never been into that. I've never been with a man in that way and never will. Their assumption is lost on me. But isn't that usually the case?

CHAPTER FORTY

Proton Therapy

DAY 54

oday is my graduation day from this self-imposed nightmare I've just endured. In the big scheme of things, fifty-four days is only a fraction of our time on earth if we're lucky. But I won't lie; the last two months have often felt like those gray, drawn-out days with the Fletchers. Only then, we didn't know when or if they would ever end. This time, I do.

Today is also my birthday. I'm certain it's no coincidence that I braved fifty-four treatments while I was fifty-four years old. I scored an early gantry time today, so I'll be finished with the final treatment by the time the clock crosses the hour of my birth.

It's not lost on me that as I turn fifty-five, I'll be handed a birthday present from the universe . . . a proverbial red box that when opened, unleashes the immeasurable potential of a fresh start, wrapped in a light almost too bright to see . . .

I am strong. I am healed. I am a warrior . . .

I miss Mom. I miss how she would hold me and go out of her way to take care of me. Even when she was sick with the cancer, she was always the nurturing one. She would be here with me now if she could. I guess she probably is in whatever way she's able . . .

If it hadn't been for her love, I don't know who I might have become. She loved and supported me through everything, even though she had inner demons she was fighting. I can't imagine how it must have torn her heart out to put us into foster care and for the Fletchers to have so much control over our visits. I guess she didn't want to rock the boat. If they refused to keep us, what would she have done?

I wish I could tell her that I empathize with the pain she must have gone through during that time. She must have felt so alone. She must have been more scared than any time in her life. But I was too young to under-stand anything about how she was feeling. I wish I could be the one to tell her that I know she did the only thing she thought she could do in that situation to take care of her family. I'm sure people looked down on her, but they weren't in her shoes. Maybe that's why she was so compassionate. She knew what it was like to be judged and she didn't want to be like that.

She always told me I didn't need a woman to be happy. She told me I was a strong and capable person who could take care of myself. She was always pumping me up like that. She was so supportive when I lived with Dan, even though she didn't know we were a couple. But she had to know. I never told her we were. But I'm sure she knew. She just loved Dan like a son and never asked any questions. Did she just not want to talk about it? Maybe she would have been uncomfortable. But if she was ashamed, why would she be so accepting? She never pushed me to date girls or said any-thing to make me question myself. So of course she had to know I liked men. I could never bring myself to tell her, but there's no way she didn't know.

I always thought she told me I didn't need a woman to be happy be-cause she didn't want me to think I needed another person to make me feel complete. I thought she didn't want me to settle. But now I can't help but wonder if telling me that was her way of giving me permission to be my-self. I always assumed she was talking in general about girlfriends and marriage, but now I think she was trying to tell me in her own way that if a man made me happy, then that was okay. I assumed I couldn't tell her the truth. And I guess she assumed she couldn't tell me directly that she was fine with whoever I loved. I can't believe I never saw it until now. All along, in her own sweet way, she was telling me I was okay. That she always believed I was perfect exactly the way I was . . .

As I left that final treatment, the staff handed me a memento: the bal-loon tube they used to push my organs away from my prostate.

"Every man receives this like a diploma," one of them said. "You are now a member of the brotherhood of men with prostate cancer."

Stunned, I said nothing.

I was not going to claim having prostate cancer. I knew now more than ever how powerful the mind was over the body. And I certainly wanted no tangible reminder of the most uncomfortable, intrusive period of my life.

I don't know what they expected me to do with that wretched piece of invasive equipment, but I did.

On the way out of the treatment center, I dumped it—and everything it signified—into the trash.

CHAPTER FORTY-ONE

Shortly after the proton therapy ended, the scans picked up nothing that resembled a tumor, and the doctors pronounced that the cancer was gone. Erupting in celebration, Bill and I indulged in a lavish dinner out, looking ahead once again at our plans for the future, as if the worst had faded into the past like a road that disappeared behind us, Alicia Keys' tunes dancing out the open windows, as we flew down a sun-soaked highway of second chances. But underneath my elation that the investment of countless hours and thousands of dollars, the consistent affirmations, and the near-daily bone-deep humiliation had all been worth it was a nagging insecurity, an unsettling taunting that the cancer could come back the way it did with my mom. I refused to give in to it, telling my internal oppressor that I didn't need that kind of reminder. But there was something else too. The threat of losing my sexuality as a result of the treatment had infused me with deep-seated vulnerability. So far, I had beat the risk. But it's the only excuse I can offer for giving in to what became an inane affair of the heart with Dylan.

Over the past couple months, I had allowed Dylan and all his baggage into my already upside-down world. I needed something to distract me from the long waits in the gantry and my anxiety of what could happen to me if the therapy didn't work, and Dylan provided that in spades.

Being a huge sports star—and fearing his fans' and society's reaction—Dylan believed he couldn't come clean about his sexual identity. He poured his heart out to me, and I did my best to encourage and support him as a friend, listening, advising, and consoling him off and on for weeks. While I always strove to stay objective and to never lead him on or cross what I thought would be an inappropriate line, it did feed my ego that he put so much faith in my opinions. He had no idea that during our exchanges, I was often trembling in an open-backed gown with a dozen other frightened men, leading a valiant crusade for my life.

Not wanting to add to his angst, I had kept the cancer a secret from Dylan. But just before my treatment ended, something prompted me to confess to him what I'd been going through. Shocked and filled with concern, he reacted by swaddling me in care and sympathy, his attachment to me growing like constricting tendrils of ivy. As his epistolary affection escalated, I knew I was walking on shaky ground—Bill had never been anything but a pillar of loving support, and now Dylan was drawing closer to me in a way that Bill would have every right to question. It didn't help that as I rejected Dylan's affections, I also secretly relished them.

Truth be told, I felt like a weak, ungrateful bastard.

Wanting both to see Dylan and to dispense any interest he might have in me by demonstrating in person how solid Bill and I were, I invited him to the US to see the paintings I had done of him for my series.

But my plan backfired.

After visiting my studio, Bill and I took Dylan on a short flight to San Francisco for a day of sightseeing. Landing in a gay bar, we proceeded to knock back several drinks as Bill and I urged Dylan to stop living a charade, persuading him that owning his truth was the best thing he could do.

"I think you'd be surprised how positive it could turn out for you," Bill said. "You might be a whole different kind of hero for being authentic."

Dylan shook his head and stirred his cocktail. "I highly doubt it. I have a reputation to uphold. And you know my family's against me coming out. They're afraid reporters will have a field day and my career will be ruined."

"You don't know that for sure," Bill said, excusing himself to use the bathroom. "Just think about it."

As soon as Bill disappeared, Dylan turned to me. His eyes pierced mine, and he grasped my hand. In that moment, he was no longer a rugby star in the UK, nor was he straight.

"I'm in love with you," he confessed, the syllables of his accent colliding like a poem. Then he leaned in and kissed me passionately.

With feelings of my own and alcohol raging through me, I didn't stop him. When he pulled away, he said, "Please, please leave Bill and come back to Wales with me."

My mind raced. "I can't do that."

"Then I'll move here. You can break things off with Bill and I'll start over here in the US."

I shook my head. "I can't. I'm sorry if I made you think it was more."

"Sorry?" Dylan blurted. "That's exactly what you made me think!"

I knew he was right. But instead of owning it, I said, "I've been your friend. That's it."

"My friend? Then what was all that stuff about? All the texts and emails?"

"It was me being your friend," I insisted.

Dylan shook his head like he couldn't believe what he was hearing. Then, like a petulant child, he yanked his hand away from mine. My heart galloped at full speed as I sat dumbfounded, then changed my expression as I saw Bill approaching.

"Everything okay?" Bill asked, his eyes darting between us.

"Everything's fine," I lied.

What the hell have I gotten myself into? I wondered.

———

After Dylan returned to Wales, we kept in touch, despite my better judgment. I convinced myself that breaking off our friendship would only serve to hurt him. And because he was prone to depression, I reasoned that I didn't want to be responsible for making it worse. So while he continued to sell himself as my meant-to-be partner—though I maintained that would never happen—I continued to let his intermittent flirtation feed my primitive, egoistic need to feel attractive to a hot, young athlete. It was pathetic, yes, but it seemed the distance between us made it safe to play our childish game.

Several months later, Dylan once again came to the States for a visit. This time, however, a music producer friend of ours was hosting a grand party at his magnificent home in Palm Springs. Being our guest, of course Dylan came with us.

The soirée was teeming with handsome, stylishly dressed men, many of whom weren't shy about making their attraction to Dylan known. But Dylan wasn't interested. The more he drank, the more his affection toward me became obvious anytime Bill was socializing or looking the other way.

Finally, my sister Noel, who had come with her husband and was standing nearby, had had enough.

"Who do you think you are," she seethed, "flirting with my brother like that? You're supposed to be his friend, not someone trying to break up his relationship!"

Dylan teetered, then became angry. "I'm in love with him!" he said too loudly.

Noel grabbed his arm but Dylan shook her off.

"You keep your voice down," she implored. "You're going to cause a scene."

"I don't care," Dylan said. "We've been in love for months!"

I glanced around, mortified. "That's a lie!"

But the people within earshot were visibly upset; Bill and I were models of fidelity among our peers, and their grimaces told me they weren't sure who to believe. By the time Bill came back to the circle, it was clear that something was terribly wrong.

He pulled me into a quiet corner. "What's up with Dylan?" Bill asked.

I shook my head and sighed. "He's drunk and making accusations about us that aren't true."

"About us? You mean, you and me?"

"No, about him and me. He's got it in his stupid head that we're more than friends."

Bill raised his eyebrows and looked straight through me. "Are you?"

"Of course not!"

Bill continued staring at me, his doubt palpable.

"He's been my muse, that's it. He thinks it's more, but it's not. It's *not.*"

Bill's suspicion coated me like papier maché, hardening with the weight of my guilt for entertaining something I knew was careless and selfish.

"Babe, I swear . . . I never meant for him to take our friendship as anything more than that."

After all Bill and I had been through—the baggage of my past, the cancer diagnosis, the weeks of treatment—it was coming down to me acting like a scared little boy in foster care, unsure if my mother would come back for me. Only I wasn't a little boy, and the situation wasn't imposed on me; I had nurtured it in my own way, for my own needs. And Bill wasn't my mother. He was my soul mate. And he deserved better than the sidelong glances and murmurs of the guests at that party. He deserved someone who didn't play with fire, not even in a brick house.

———

A few months later, splashed all over the Internet, was the news that one of Europe's most celebrated rugby stars had come out as gay.

For two weeks, Dylan didn't so much as send a friendly text about his decision. But it wasn't because of media backlash or disparagement from his fans or even his family that he stayed out of touch. He was still angry with me for not caving to an affair—or better, leaving Bill and my entire life behind to start a life with him. It was then that I realized I had nurtured our friendship for multiple reasons: to be a support system for Dylan, yes; and to feed my own ego, yes; but I also stayed in it because as long as I did, he couldn't abandon me, which had always been the one damaged part of me I couldn't seem to repair.

As Dylan's fame rose and his role model status escalated just as we suspected it would, he rode the wave as a media darling, shunning both Bill and me.

And I, in my perpetual state of self-loathing for fostering our indiscriminate friendship, not only lamented the feeling of abandonment that mocked me like a bully on the playground, but invited the one thing back into my life I hoped I had conquered.

CHAPTER FORTY-TWO

2011

Stress feeds cancer like the sun feeds nature. It's neither personal nor arbitrary; both are simply doing what's intrinsic to them. Only the sun has the noblest of intentions, while stress beelines it straight to the vulnerable places, laughing at how you invited it in, how you did nothing to stop it.

If someone had asked me to define my particular source of stress, one so great that it caused my body to rebel and reignite the cancer, I would be hard-pressed to come up with a single answer. I could have called it Dylan, but that would be unfair. What it really was was a string of unpleasant adjectives that all described me:

Dishonest. Indulgent. Reckless. Selfish. Needy. Puerile.

The perfect ingredients to welcome graffiti back into my body where once the slate was clean.

In a nutshell, the next few years of my life weren't driving down that open highway of possibility, the warm breeze and benevolent sun kissing our future. Instead, it was a series of swerves and stops, inclement weather and unpredicted detours.

But it was also peppered with nature's magic, resonant lyrics, unexpected clearings, roadside wonders.

And Bill.

Despite the fact that I almost lost him over my non-consummated, yet foolhardy foray into infantilism—and despite the fact that once he discovered the truth about Dylan's feelings for me and how I had unwittingly fostered them, he would have had every right to leave—somehow, he found it in his heart to stay.

In that humbling pocket of reconciliation that followed the madness, I realized I didn't know what was real and what wasn't during my connection with Dylan. I also realized that it didn't matter. What mattered was Bill.

My stalwart mountain, my ray of light.

I had been terribly careless to jeopardize the remarkable life we had built together. The chaotic strokes of black that coated that time in my life would be difficult for both of us to scrape away. But although it took some time to heal, miraculously, those missteps resulted in an even stronger bond between us.

I may not have deserved it, but in the mist and the sludge and the drought and the storm, always, always, there was Bill.

Between 2011 and 2014, the scenes of my life's film reel that were related to cancer flashed on the screen in a clipped montage that looked something like this:

Having already had radiation for prostate cancer—which means you can't then have surgery—my previous treatment center refused me as a patient.

My oncologist sent me to a urologist performing experimental procedures, who removed lymph nodes from my groin, five of which were positive for cancer.

Choosing to do nothing, I waited a year while my doctor kept an eye on my PSA scores.

During this time, my doctor discovered that the cancer had metastasized to my bones as well as my lymph nodes, labeling it stage IV.

When my PSA scores increased, I went on hormone suppression therapy, which essentially drained my body of testosterone using a drug called Lupron, causing me to experience male menopause, complete with depression, hot flashes, bone loss, weight gain, and a libido that plummeted to zero. But it also brought my PSA scores back down to normal.

Refusing to rely solely on Western medicine, I cleaned up my diet, cut back on drinking, tapped deeper into my spiritual self, and recited meaningful affirmations of health and well-being daily, all of which enhanced my quality of life. I also amped up my already steady, six-days-a-week workout sessions, augmenting the weight-bearing exercises to benefit my bones.

Open to a new method of obliterating the cancer, I entered a clinical trial for an immune-enhancing therapy with the use of an experimental drug called Provenge, wherein they take a good portion of your blood, reprocess it with Provenge, then reintroduce that blood into your body a week later.

I did so well on the Provenge therapy that I went off all other drugs I'd been taking, including the Lupron.

In short, I was a model patient for my oncologist. She had told me, "You worry about being strong, and I'll worry about keeping you healthy." And together, that formula seemed to be working.

But then, my PSA scores began to rise again. While multiple factors can cause that, theoretically, it happens when testosterone is present. In my case, however—despite being off the hormone-suppressing drug—my testosterone level had remained virtually nonexistent.

Perplexed, I felt it was time to do something radical—and shockingly, my oncologist supported me.

CHAPTER FORTY-THREE

2014

I have never been attached to any particular religion. But I've always believed in a higher power, and especially during the time of the cancer treatment, I'd been a seeker of truth and inspiration from people and teachings of various faiths and ideologies.

Through reading numerous books and articles, as well as watching videos and interviews, I had at some point been introduced to the man called John of God. Residing in Abadiânia, Brazil, and considered a "psychic surgeon" among other monikers, he is one of the most famous faith healers in the world; celebrities and wellness leaders—such Oprah and Wayne Dyer— have hailed his abilities miraculous. But he has also been called a charlatan, making him highly controversial among people of science, and even of faith. As a seemingly anointed man who facilitates the healing of people afflicted with any number of maladies, he has been quoted as saying:

> I do not cure anybody. God heals, and in His infinite goodness permits the entities to heal and console my brothers. I am merely an instrument in God's Divine hands.

Intrigued by what appeared to be John of God's extraordinary gift, my curiosity was further piqued after seeing an episode of *Oprah's Next Chapter* that featured him. On that show, a woman named Heather discussed making thrice-yearly pilgrimages to Brazil with a small group. Immediately drawn to the idea, and with Bill's blessing, I made it my mission to contact her and secure a spot for Bill, me, and our dear friend Luke to see if I might receive healing once and for all.

Serendipitously, my outreach was successful, and Bill and Luke—though admittedly skeptical—agreed to accompany Heather, along with twenty-six other hopefuls, on a trip to Brazil with me in the summer.

Now, I won't lie. The thought of being in the presence of this man, to whom thousands of people flocked each day—and who performed open surgeries on people with no anesthetic, and astoundingly, with little to no pain inflicted on them—induced overpowering nerves in me. But I also knew that the odds of us being part of Heather's group were slim to none, and the fact that we were had to signify that my healing was imminent— and without a doubt meant to be.

When we arrived in Abadiânia, it felt akin to Jews lining the Wailing Wall of Jerusalem, or Muslims making the hajj to Mecca. Scores of eager-to-be-healed people from all over the world swarmed the vicinity as we were escorted to the modest, yet lovely digs where we would stay, similar to a primitive hotel.

As we settled in, Heather asked each of us to take some time to write down our intentions for being there. In a couple of days, when John of God would be present, she would give these pieces of paper to him. It wasn't clear if he would base his chosen healings on these intentions, but we all took it seriously nonetheless.

Two days later, amongst the reverent whispers and chanting of the throng, John of God slowly made his way through us to the stage where he would bring individuals up for healing. Somehow, we had obtained front-row status, so it was easy to see that he was a simple man, with no air of pretense or televangelical tendencies. In fact, we were told that we must not see him as God or in any way divine, that he was merely a conduit who channeled various doctors from the other side, and then took their "advice" on how to heal whatever ailed that particular person.

Being in the front row afforded another perk: if John of God looked you in the eyes and reached out his hand, it meant you had been chosen. That is, of course, if fear didn't make you look away.

John of God locked eyes on me twice and reached toward me, and both times, I looked away.

I couldn't help it; I was uneasy, and averting my eyes was my reflex. As a result, he moved on to other people who weren't terrified of being cut open onstage or having him otherwise manipulate their bodies to achieve their desired outcome.

As I watched him perform varied types of surgeries for hours, after which the individuals were taken to "ICU"—which was their term for remaining isolated in your room for twenty-four hours in order to fully heal—I wondered if we had come all this way only to be fascinated observers.

It would be three more days before I'd find out.

On the fifth day of the trip, all of us had been experiencing our own versions of healing, whether it was spiritual, physical, emotional, or mental; simply being there inspired deep introspection. We had also been taking the pills John of God "prescribed" and his many helpers dispensed, which were a blend of special herbs that he had blessed with his healing intentions. Everybody received different types of pills, depending on what John of God sensed you needed. It was all quite unorthodox and mysterious, but it was also all part of the mystical experience.

On that particular evening, Heather felt certain that a profound healing process had been set in motion for me, and I was sent to ICU for it to properly take place. Settled in for my twenty-four hours of isolation in my room with Bill and Luke, I didn't feel anything specific.

Until I awoke around midnight.

Gripped by a searing pain, as if taken over by a force to rid my body of something vile, I dashed to the bathroom and began throwing up so fiercely that I could barely stand the intensity of the retching. Within minutes, the vomiting wasn't enough; diarrhea surged from me so quickly that I didn't know which way to position myself. Bolts rippled through me as if I was being struck repeatedly by lightning, as I hurled and excreted years of secrets and lies, heartache and shame, remorse and guilt. Never had I felt so sick or been in so much agony, not even when I was hit by the car when I was eleven, or had put my arm through the glass door, practically severing my hand. For seven incomprehensible hours, the dark parts of my life were wrung out of me from every orifice, leaving me begging God to make it stop. As soon as I sent up my petition, the purging ceased like a tornado suddenly dissipating into the sky after leaving miles of destruction. I felt like a caterpillar who had been reduced to his soupy liquid inside the chrysalis, awaiting fortification to emerge as a butterfly.

Bill and Luke had spent their entire night tending to me and repeatedly cleaning up the mess. The sounds that had emanated from me for hours had made everyone in our group assume that the majority of us had food poisoning, or some equally caustic bug. But it turned out that what had sounded like the collective illness of thirty people was caused only by me.

When morning arrived, Bill and Luke checked in with Heather, who told them to hydrate me with coconut water, then allow me to rest as long as I needed to. When I woke up, I could come down for a small meal.

Seven hours later, I awoke feeling slightly drained, but also light and renewed. The protocol was to wear all white each day of the trip to signify that you came with a pure heart and desired healing. But after my night of trauma, I couldn't imagine enduring any more healing, so I showed up for my meal wearing black. With a smile, Heather patted my arm and told me to change back into white.

"The spirits know you don't need more healing of that nature," she said. "But you've come a long way to have this experience, so I want you to stay open to whatever may happen here for you."

Believing she'd experienced this enough times to put my trust in her, I changed back into white and awaited whatever God had in store for me.

The next several days were moving but uneventful in terms of palpable transformations or epiphanies. But on day eleven, Heather took us to a site where gorgeous sacred waterfalls have been believed for centuries to catalyze healing. I had no idea what to expect, but believing I was done with painful purging, and knowing we were leaving the next day, I embraced the beauty and opportunity with no expectations.

Encouraged to wade in and immerse ourselves, Bill, Luke, and I marveled at the clear blue water and the magical feeling it seemed to instill to be steeped in it. After about an hour, I didn't feel anything but grateful for the experience—no internal shift, no revelations, and certainly no painful stirrings.

Patting myself dry, I was reflecting on my sense of gratitude when something bright and almost ethereal appeared in front of me. I blinked hard and realized that a blue morpho butterfly was fluttering close enough for me to touch. Because they're indigenous to the rainforests of Latin America, I'd never seen one in person before—or at least not this close—and I almost couldn't believe it was real. With its bright blue wings edged with black, the blue morpho is one of the largest butterflies in the world, with wings spanning from five to eight inches. The microscopic scales on the backs of their wings create a vivid, iridescent blue coloring that reflects light, while the underside of its wings is a dull brown with numerous eyespots that provide camouflage against predators when its wings are closed. This combination results in pure magic: when the blue morpho flies, the contrasting bright blue and dull brown colors flash, making it look like it's appearing and disappearing.

For several moments, as if suspended in time, the blue morpho and I communed as one connected being. It was in that sacred pocket of time that I truly understood that everything in our universe is connected, that any sense of separation between us is only an illusion. I had read this, and even believed it, but until that blue morpho came to teach me the lesson in person, I hadn't sincerely *felt* it. That butterfly could have been my mother set free, or even the embodiment of the cancer leaving me. Whatever it represented—and I knew it could be numerous things—I sensed deep within, like the transmuted caterpillar, that I would never be the same.

CHAPTER FORTY-FOUR

After we came home from Brazil, I could sense that I was continuing to heal. It's difficult to explain in words, but I felt that my mind, body, and spirit were being reshaped from the experience of being in the presence of John of God, and in the magical environment of Abadiânia. Within forty days, though I had had no tests to prove it, I had an overwhelming feeling that the cancer in my body was gone. I also felt what I can only describe as a profound faith in the entities of Love and Light, and the complete loss of my fear of death.

With my newfound calm also came the knowledge that my health wasn't something I could ever take for granted. I had already recovered from the last injury to my hand, with my artistic ability remarkably preserved. And I knew I couldn't make any assumptions about being cured or immune from future bouts of cancer—or any other dis-ease for that matter. So I chose to go to an integrative clinic for protocols that were not only proven effective for reducing inflammation, and therefore keeping my immune system at its optimum, but that were also known to be cancer inhibitors. In essence, I did everything I could to keep the miraculous self-healing mechanisms we are born with in tip-top shape, including vitamin C infusions, eliminating processed foods and refined sugar, and having oxygen therapy sessions and thermogenic treatments. I also practiced meditation and profound gratitude, and continued reciting daily health and well-being affirmations, which I truly believed were as important as anything physical I was doing to keep myself well.

As is typical when a person straddles Western and integrative protocols, my integrative doctor wanted me off all prescription meds, but my oncologist didn't necessarily agree. So, as a patient, I had to make decisions based on what I believed was instinctually right for me. While that's not a perfect science by any means, I had learned over the past several years—and especially in Brazil—to listen to my body more than to people in white coats, and I had come to a place where my deep connection with all things allowed me to more strongly trust the language in which my body spoke to me. Sometimes this meant I embarked on a new clinical trial; other times it meant saying no to a procedure that didn't sit right with me. Still other times it meant staying on a drug while using natural methods alongside it. But always it meant getting quiet, asking the universe for guidance, and listening.

Several months later, my integrative doctor recommended that I have a stem cell transplant in my prostate, which had proven promising for cancer patients like me. My prostate showed no signs of a tumor, but my pubic bone and a few lymph nodes did. The hope was that the stem cells would systemically attack the cancer that was residing there. After meditating on it, I felt good about moving forward, passed all the tests, and had the procedure.

Within months, however, as a shock to all of us, my PSA scores rose higher than ever, which signified that the cells were multiplying, releasing a prostate-specific antigen in my blood. It was impossible to know what had caused it; it was unlikely that it was the stem cells, so my doctors and I didn't believe we'd made a wrong decision there. But I was still faced with a new dilemma. A cutting-edge drug helped reduce my PSA level, but the integrative clinic thought it best that I travel to an innovative radiologist/oncologist in San Diego, California, to have the pubic bone tumor removed.

To be honest, I wasn't thrilled with the idea. I didn't particularly want to put myself in the hands of yet another new doctor, but I chose to trust the recommendation and traveled the fifty miles just the same. But after administering the anesthetic and making his best effort, the doctor couldn't reach the tumor without potentially damaging other organs, so he closed me up without performing the surgery.

Afterward, he told Bill and me that he wanted me to return for a procedure where he would freeze the tumor with a cryogenic technique. After he explained the pros and cons—emphasizing the pros—I reluctantly agreed but said I wanted to discuss it with my other oncologist before deciding for sure. When I did, she said there was no way to freeze the tumor, based on where it was located, without potential damage to my colon. To say that red flags were set off in both of us was an understatement.

The truth is, two doctors can see things very differently, and while we don't want science to be read on a sliding scale, sometimes it simply is. In this case, I trusted my oncologist's opinion more than I trusted this new doctor, so I emailed to tell him that I wasn't sure about the cryogenic surgery after all and that I wanted to wait.

A couple of weeks later, I received a call to confirm my surgery, which was slated for the next day.

"But I sent you an email," I said. "I never said I had decided to do it."

"I never got an email," he snapped. "We can't cancel now. I've already flown other doctors in to assist at great expense."

My mouth hung open. Though I sympathized with his predicament, he seemed to have no regard for my wishes as his patient. That's when I sensed I was likely going to be a guinea pig of sorts and my intuition sounded off.

"But that's not my fault," I said. "There was no communication from you."

I was right and he knew it. But instead of acknowledging that, he went off on me, blaming me for setting the procedure in motion and inconveniencing multiple people. When I realized there was no chance of having a rational conversation around the mixup, I made up a quick lie.

"I'm sorry," I said, "but I'm also sick." I let out the most realistic-sounding coughs I could. "I have a pretty nasty cold."

He got quiet, so quiet that I wondered if he was trying to measure my cough on his bullshit meter. "Fine," he finally said. "We can't operate on you if you're sick. It's a huge inconvenience, but I suppose we can reschedule."

But I knew for a fact that I wasn't going to reschedule and told him as much. He tried to persuade me, but I stood firm. He may have thought he could freeze the tumor without consequence, but I wasn't about to risk my ability to defecate without a bag attached to me for the rest of my life to find out.

———

For most people, living with stage IV cancer might sound like a death sentence. Thriving with that diagnosis may even seem impossible. But for me, it simply meant I hadn't yet cracked the code of why these foreign invaders had taken up residence in my body. Being railroaded by fear was not an option for me; being my own best advocate was.

Not only did I refuse to be intimidated by doctors who used scare tactics to push me into procedures, but I used multiple means as therapy for my soul, which I knew could heal me as readily as—if not more than—any new drug or innovative strategy.

First, I utilized myriad holistic conventions to support my body's self-healing mechanisms. Besides those I've already mentioned, I took epsom salt baths, had colonics, partook in BioMat sessions, drank hydrogen water, supplemented with natural anti-inflammatories, such as high doses of turmeric, started my day with lemon and ginger water, ate a mostly ketogenic diet, and used cannabis, among other means.

Second, I was committed to living in a high-vibrational state of peace, calm, and love, in whatever way that manifested for me—through my art, my friendships, my self-care, my relationship with Bill, and my connection to God and the universe.

For the next two years of my life, this is how I lived, and this is how I thrived, with stage IV cancer.

CHAPTER FORTY-FIVE

I chew on my nails, a nervous habit I've never broken, waiting for the receptionist to call my name. It is January 21, 2017, and I am my oncologist's first patient of the day.

My doctor welcomes me into her office and hugs me, tells me that she's just arrived, then sits and scans her computer screen with the results of my recent blood draw. The last several checks have been fine, and there's no reason to believe this one will be different. Yet it is only seconds before I see the minute change in her face, that shift from clinical to compassionate, as she closes her eyes for a moment and turns to me.

She sighs and her shoulders fall. "I know you've worked really hard, Paul," she says, softly shaking her head and placing her hand on my knee. "I'm sorry."

There is no doubt that this is a blow.

But although my eyes well with tears, I know this is merely a bump in the road.

Am I tired of bumps? *Yes.*

Have I weathered them before? *Yes.*

Am I stronger, more resilient, and more compassionate because of them? *Yes.*

The truth is, cancer doesn't define a person, and one must never own it as theirs. I know I don't. It is merely a temporary resident, a symptom that something is awry in the body. That something can be because of a reckless lifestyle, poor eating habits, too much alcohol, exposure to chemicals, ingestion of GMOs, environmental factors, prescription medications, the list goes on. It can also be from emotional wounds and past hurts, unforgiven acts, resentments, and regrets, secrets and lies. With all of these elements so prevalent in most of our lives, it's almost a wonder anyone is well.

But that's the miracle of the human body.

I'm now sixty-five years old. Some may say that some form of dis-ease was inevitable for me by now. But I say that's not true. Had I done better for myself sooner, I believe I could have prevented getting cancer. I am certainly an advocate for living well in every way possible—physically, mentally, emotionally, and spiritually—so that dis-ease has no opportunity to take up residence in the body. When you're armed with the knowledge of how to care beautifully for yourself and actually do it, it's entirely possible—and even desired by the universe—to live without illness, no matter your age. And I unequivocally recommend that over trying to backpedal and heal an illness that's already set in.

Me? I didn't have all the tools then that I have now, but I do know this:

I believe in the diagnosis but not the prognosis.

It is always best to dwell in positive, not negative, thoughts, because thoughts have an energy all their own that affect the body, the mind, and everything and everyone around us.

Love and faith will always trump fear.

Cancer is *not* a death sentence.

Forgiving everybody of everything, including yourself, is the greatest portal to freedom.

Life is a series of decisions that shape you. What may seem like a mistake or regret is meant to teach you something valuable and elevate your soul, so seek to glean the nugget of wisdom. Don't be too hard on yourself. At the same time, do your best not to inflict suffering on others, whether human or animal. We are all God's creatures, all created from the same spark of Divine intelligence, and therefore connected and precious.

The path isn't always clear, the message not always immediately understood or welcome. But you can choose to be a beacon of light, or you can choose to cast a shadow.

The universe truly *is* on our side.

———

At this point in my life, cancer is still a temporary resident in my body. But I will never claim it as permanent, nor will I let it frighten me into submission.

I am strong. I am healthy. I am a warrior.

My latest artistic series is called Warriors with Messengers, where I address death as part of humans' fate and as the beginning of a new journey, not as the end of our existence. The question, *What happens when we die?* is one of the greatest mysteries of humanity. I know first-hand how frightening it can be to think about our own mortality, which is why I've endeavored to give a positive spin on the premise.

Inspired by my stay in Brazil, I created eight life-size white sculptures—with objects from different places of origin—not only to present death as a blank canvas, but also as a tribute to friends and family who died battling cancer. Every sculpture represents one person and is named with one of the predominant attributes I observed in them: Love, Compassion, Perseverance, Nature, Knowledge, Strength, Passion, and Hope. Every warrior shares a message of life and a virtue we should strive to preserve, while the white texture invites the observer to think about the possibility of new beginnings, as well as the purity of death as part of life itself.

I dreamed of a better life—perhaps even a life infused with a bit of magic—as I pumped myself higher, higher on the swings as a child.

The canvas started out in smears of unease, spatters of uncertainty. But over time, brushed with the colors of love, loss, self-awareness, and wisdom, it has become—and continues to evolve into—a boy dreamer's perfectly imperfect version of a masterpiece.

⌒✺⌒

To You, Dear Mom,

Although my years with you were short, and I didn't get to have you as long as I would have liked, our deep connection was a rare treasure that was way beyond our years. It's still hard to believe that you were only forty-nine when you passed, leaving me in my early twenties to figure out life without you. I must admit, I was not the same after you left me. Even years later, there are still countless moments when I find myself saying, "I wish you were here."

I lost much more than just you when you left, and I miss you more than words could ever explain. I miss your smile, I miss your laugh, I miss your hugs, I miss the way you looked at me with pride. There are so many things I wanted to share with you and could not.

You asked me as I held your hand on your deathbed if I was gay, and I said no because I was ashamed and didn't want to disappoint you—even though I knew your love for me was unconditional and that you wanted me to be happy. I know now that you also asked so that I could move on; you wanted to help free me and lessen my load, but I just couldn't admit the truth, not even to you.

You took so much pride in me, and I always knew, even in the hardest of times, that you loved me with all your heart. I also see, as I get older, why you taught me so many of the things you did. You left an indelible imprint on me, and you never let me slack on becoming the person you knew I was capable of being. You always saw my potential and believed in me, even when I didn't believe in myself. Your being my number-one fan meant more to me than you will ever know.

Losing you has taught me so much—it taught me that life is temporary and to value and appreciate each and every day. It taught me what real love truly is and that life is precious. It taught me, too, what real pain and loss feels like, but also what it means to have purpose.

No matter where life takes me, I will always take a part of you with me. I promised to make you proud of me, and I will continue striving—with every decision and step I take for the rest of my life—to honor you and to be the best version of the son you loved so much.

Thank you for being the most loving, giving, compassionate, and understanding mom. You told me all the time that I could and would accomplish whatever I worked at and put my mind to, and I hope I've fulfilled your dreams for me as you've watched me from your place in heaven.

I love you, Paul

GALLERY

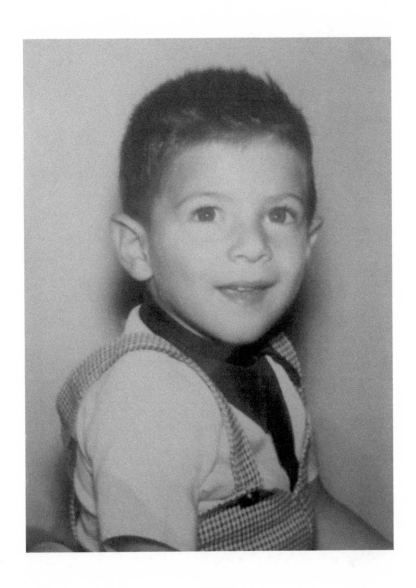

Me, age three

Me, Mom, and Gail, 1956

Tina and Noel,
circa 1965

Me, Gail,
Tina, and Noel
Sea World, San Diego,
circa 1967

Mom and Dad in happier times

One of my favorite starlet photos of Mom

Bill and me, 2017

———

Hohmann Gallery, Palm Desert, CA
Fractal Series
2018

WARRIORS WITH MESSENGERS
MESSENGER MEANINGS

Butterflies are deep and powerful representations of life.
Many cultures associate the butterfly with our souls.
The Christian religion sees the butterfly as a symbol of
resurrection. Around the world, people view the butterfly as
representing endurance, change, hope, and life.

Bird spirit is the perfect symbol for freedom and
perspective. Because they fly high into the sky,
Lightworkers often tell us that they are messengers of the
Gods who provide humans with a bridge between the
mundane and spiritual life.

*(left) Virtue of Love
Representing my beloved
mom, holding both a
butterfly and birds*

*(below) All eight
Warriors with
Messengers
taken in my studio
2018*

ACKNOWLEDGMENTS

My deepest gratitude to the following people:

My editor/gifted and talented writer Stacey Aaronson. More than a writer and editor, Stacey proved to be a reassuring force and confidante, completely committed to making me proud of my memoir. She really should have shared the platform with me, but she refused. My dear Stacey, I am so proud of *Boy Dreamer*. Thank you.

Bill, my loving partner of forty years, who has completely supported and encouraged me to write my story. I have truly been blessed with our relationship and love you deeply.

My family, who was instrumental in gathering factual information—in particular, my older sister, Gail. I couldn't have written this book without them. Tina and Laura, I love you. Evan, my brother, I wish I knew you better and hope I do someday.

My genius oncologist, Tanya Dorff, who has helped keep me healthy and my quality of life intact.

My friends who have taught me many lessons, always been honest, and always embraced me. Laura Markarian, my dear and close friend, who has always been there for me and never judged me. Patrick Stanton, who has traveled the world with us and has always been a dedicated confidant and loyal friend. JP Malric, with whom I have a divine understanding and shared language—kindred spirits we are. Chad Halsey, you are so dear to me. Benoit Fosse and Vincent Bennett, two of my healers. Virginia Repasky, my art agent, thank you for guiding my career. Norma Samuelson, I am so grateful for your friendship and your artistic ability. Your illustrations for my children's book, *Root the Noot Goot*, are beyond creative. Author Gregg Seller, you inspired me to write *Boy Dreamer*. Mitchell Hollander and Michael Mooney, who have been incredibly supportive in too many ways to mention. Patty and Steve Carlson, who have made life more interesting with their creative talents and the unconditional love they have shown. PJ, who listened, gave her opinion, and set me straight. Estella Rubin, James Shilaimon, Patricia Lax, Yvette Jacobson. Deb Conery, my childhood friend who saw the Broadway Village completely differently. Leslie Marchetti, who gave me my start in the art world in her Fine Art Gallery in La Jolla, CA. Mike Conley, Gary LeFebvre, Marc Sanders, Pasquale Bettino, Robin Main, Robyn Kaufman, Roger Canevari, Darrell Brown, Dave Mayo, Joost Bosch and Petro Hermans, Brad and Kristeia Ahmic, and Reg Kercelus, good friends who have been there for me always. And to the many very dear friends I know I've left out, thank you for your friendships.

Glenn Cram and Alvin Morrison, two souls who have passed, who were monumental in my development and spiritually guided me with their wisdom and love. My love for you will never end, just as the sun never refuses to shine on the world.

My surrogate daughter, Iona, who I love with all my heart and soul.

Noel, my youngest sister, you are my rock. I love you.

Jeffrey O'Connor, I love you deeply as a friend and partner, and I treasure your kind and giving ways. You are very special to me. I have embraced our journey together.

Carol Meyer, it started with you believing in me. Thank you!

Seven friends who generously agreed to read the entire manuscript and offer their wise critiques: Patrick Stanton, PJ LaBarge, Laura Markarian, Gary LeFebvre, Chad Halsey, Jeffrey O'Connor, and Bill Merrill.

I have been given many gifts, but the biggest gift is life. Thank you Mom and Dad. I love you both.

ABOUT THE BOOK

ABOUT THE AUTHOR

PARTING INSPIRATION

M
O
R
E

with

PAUL
ECKE

A
B
O
U
T

t h e

B
O
O
K

1. Though Paul was only in foster care for fifteen months, how did incidents that occurred there impact his entire life?

2. What messages did you as a reader take away with regard to the influence that adults' words and actions have on children? Which scenes in the book lent to those opinions?

3. What emotions or thoughts came up for you around Paul's mother? Did you find yourself judging her? If so, were you also able to have compassion for her? Why or why not?

4. Society's "rules" can be unreasonably damaging, particularly for those whose sexual identity isn't widely supported or understood. How did those restrictions force Paul into hiding who he really was? Do you think they were influenced by his growing up in the 60s and 70s? Do you think it may have been different for him growing up today?

5. In what ways did you witness Paul creating façades? Why do you think he felt the need to do this, both as a child and as an adult?

6. Paul displayed profound sensitivity and creativity as a child that he often kept inside. Have you experienced keeping traits or talents hidden because you weren't supported in being your authentic self?

7. Paul had several accidents and near-death experiences in his young life. What meaning did you attach to them? Do you relate to any of them in terms of your own life?

8. Paul described himself as a "young man who was told it was wrong to be who he was, while it felt equally wrong to try to be someone else." Discuss how this relates to people marginalized in our society. Can you step into their shoes?

9. Paul held out hope that Dan would change, despite the growing volatility of their relationship. Why do you think so many people in abusive partnerships do this?

10. What decisions did Paul make as a young adult that saddened you? That shocked you? Did you relate to or empathize with the reasons he made those decisions?

11. Paul reflects on his diagnosis of cancer being a result of holding emotional stress and wounds. Do you agree? How do you think a person could remedy that?

12. Discuss the challenges that come both with hiding one's sexuality and living authentically. Have you ever been faced with a similar conflict?

13. Paul uses his proton therapy sessions as a time of deep reflection. What did you take from his reflections? Have you ever been pushed into deep introspection because of a negative event?

14. Paul lists a number of things in the final chapter that he believes to be true. Do you find encouragement, or perhaps even a new perspective, in this list? If so, how?

15. Resilience plays a dominant role in Paul's life. In what ways were you inspired by that resilience, and where did you feel it came from?

A
B
O
U
T

t h e

B
O
O
K

16. Paul bared his soul in *Boy Dreamer*, in the hope that his honesty would shed light on the following topics:

- How to find strength and courage in the face of adversity
- Lessons learned from a dysfunctional childhood defined by trauma
- How the pursuit of art can heal one's soul
- How to thrive with cancer and have the right focus on mind-body-spirit
- The challenges that are often faced in embracing one's sexual identity
- The importance of cultivating our God-given gifts
- Discovering one's truth and courageously living it

Discuss these topics and any others you found to be strong messages in the book.

PAUL ECKE, a former educator, has been a professional artist for over three decades. He is a painter of contemporary non-figurative and figurative works on canvas and panel. His works are an amalgam of color, texture, and movement achieved through application of oil and acrylic paints to canvas, all applied by brush, hand, and even trowel. The results are colorful thought- and emotion-provoking images that convey the inner strength, conviction, and complexity of the artist.

After pursuing a career teaching art in the California public school system, he headed the entire district's art program. Ecke enjoyed his nine years as an educator but longed to pursue a full-time career in the creation of his own art.

Ecke has been a full-time contributor to the contemporary art world since 1985. His works are in the collections of the Metropolitan Museum of Art, Manila, Philippines; the Crocker Museum of Art, Sacramento, California; and the Museum of Arts and Sciences in Daytona, Florida. He has shown in galleries in New York, Chicago, San Diego, Palm Springs, Florida, the Philippines, and Indonesia. His works are in many private and corporate collections, including those of Universal Studios, Jimmy Z Sportswear, Taco Bell, Flojet Corporation, Carsey Warner Productions, and Dionne Warwick's collection. Works by Paul Ecke are already slated to be part of an endowment of contemporary paintings and graphic art to the Tate Museum of Contemporary Art in London. He has been the featured artist in numerous publications, including: *Los Angeles Times*, *International Fine Art Collector Magazine*, *Space Magazine*, and *California Homes and Gardens*.

He was educated at California State University, Fullerton, receiving a degree in art with an emphasis in ceramic arts and painting.

A CONVERSATION WITH PAUL ECKE

What inspired you to pen your memoir, *Boy Dreamer*?

I had a long-held desire to understand my personal history. Having come from a fragmented home, I sought to understand the details of my childhood and how it might have affected me as an adult. So many of those memories had been suppressed and stuffed away, and making sense of them helped me to understand my adult self. Sharing these memories with my siblings also helped me to put these feelings into order and perspective. I felt I had a story to tell and had a strong desire to share it with others to hopefully inspire people through my journey.

What challenges did you overcome to pen the book?

Beginning to reflect on and write down distinct events of my life was the most difficult and humbling experience I have ever had. Reliving my life from my earliest memories, which I had never shared before, wasn't easy. Plus, I'm an artist, not a writer. I am grateful for the talented and gifted writer Stacey Aaronson who channeled me and helped bring this compelling story to fruition. She told my story and delivered it in a way no other could. I now feel it is a literary work of art.

What life lessons do you share with readers?

(A) One can overcome adversity. (B) It is possible to create the life you desire. (C) Cancer is a journey and does not have to be a death sentence. (D) Positive thinking makes the journey more bearable. (E) Positive friends and family are of ultimate importance. (F) Education opened many doors for me. (G). Having trust and faith in a higher power gave me hope. (H) I learned, after hiding my true self for so long, that sexual preference is just one element of a person.

The early chapters in your book describe in detail your time in foster care. How were you able to come out of that situation to live a fulfilling life?

Foster care was a short time in my life, but it was during early childhood when the anatomic brain structures that govern personality traits, learning processes, and coping with stress and emotions are established, strengthened, and made permanent. For this reason, I was probably underdeveloped in my emotional and coping skills in my younger years. As a result, I have had to overcome, or overcompensate, for many of my issues from foster care. I have sought out various therapies, associated myself with positive and nurturing people in my life, worked on myself through spiritual teachings, and practiced positive affirmations. I have learned the tools that help guide me to a happy and successful life, and I have a strong belief that we have the ability to create whatever we want in life. I also believe that most things happen for a reason —it's our journey, and we take the challenges that life presents to us and learn from them. Ultimately, we have choices, and we decide if we are going to be happy or not.

Your tale reveals a theme of how one lives their truth. How does one come to discover and then live their truth?

You find out what your truth is through living your life and finding out what registers with you and your authentic self. I learn more through mistakes; in fact, I now know that I have learned more from my mistakes than I ever have from my successes. Trial and error has always been my process. I have to take every situation step by step: whether it be nutrition, diet, exercise, or medical treatment. When looked at in its entirety, any goal can be overwhelming, but when broken down into steps, it becomes manageable.

***Boy Dreamer* sheds insight on you becoming a full-time artist. What drives someone to become an artist?**

I think the need to create has been there for as long as I can remember. The positive feedback I've received from each simple piece of art has encouraged me to dig deeper and to create again. When I create, I get lost in time; my body and mind transport to another place. The feeling I get is addictive and I constantly want more.

How would you describe your art?

Most of my art is abstract paintings. I also create figurative sculpture and large textural pieces. My objective is to capture the eye of the viewer and for them to want to come closer and explore the detail that each piece possesses. When this happens, I feel the piece is successful. To me every color, element, pattern, texture, and composition means something concrete or definable to the viewer. When I combine these elements, I create a piece that has a specific overall meaning to me personally. My hope is that each piece will be viewed and interpreted uniquely by the viewer. In addition, my art pieces rarely feel finished. When I leave the piece and come back to it days later, I always see that more can be done. It is not until my artist advocate photographs the piece that I agree not to revisit it.

What do you hope your art does for others?

I hope that my art creates dialogue—even between viewers of the same piece. My intention is to elicit a response: negative or positive. My subjective work is more literal or suggestive, but I still aim to stimulate thought and conversation. My desire is that my work brings enjoyment, or at least provokes emotion. Art is highly personal, and it is also subjective. For that reason, I am not here to educate people on what is considered "good art" or not.

You had trauma, drama, and family dysfunction in your childhood. How did these experiences drive your artistry?

As a young child, art was an escape from the painful situations I endured. I learned that through art, I experienced pleasure from what I created and the responses of those around me. The pain-to-pleasure that I experienced as a child creating art transferred to a pleasure-to-pleasure experience as an adult.

Does your art help keep you alive?

Art has been my escape and passion since I was a child. Whether using my imagination to create an escape, an imaginary friend, or a physical piece of art, the result was a creative response to the situation. I still feel I have more "paintings" in my mind that I will never get onto a canvas. This drives me each and every day to get up and create.

You say that art is a reflection of the artist. How so?

I believe all true art is a mirror of the artist's mind. If you know that, bear it in mind when looking at art, and your eyes will be alert for the visual details that convey it. The arts can also be a reflection of our culture and time. Because art is an individual means of expression, it is a source of beauty, communication, reflection, and pride. It is important, certainly, to communicate through words, but communication through images, sounds, and objects seems to fulfill an important human need too.

As an art teacher in the public school system, how did you seek to inspire young minds?

My goal was to inspire the minds of my students by being a living example. I encouraged each and every student to observe

A

B

O

U

T

the

A

U

T

H

O

R

closely, think critically, and discuss respectfully. I presented my curriculum to them and had them observe and translate their thoughts into language and listen and respond to multiple perspectives. My approach to teaching a class was to ask three questions to the young students: What's going on in this painting, drawing, or sculpture? What do you see that makes you say that? What more can we find? We have to be able to look at the image and understand it—or not—not just react to it. I found that most students could successfully accomplish this regardless of their creative ability in the physical application of art. Because I promoted art to my students in a non-threatening environment, they were always given positive reinforcement when they explored art projects.

You also show how one can forgive and accept parental missteps. What advice do you have for those growing up under challenging circumstances?

That's a hard one to answer. Everyone is so different and processes things differently. I believe I had a gift, which was my imaginative and creative mind. It afforded me the ability to dream and to transport myself to happier places when things at home got rough. I knew at a very early age that I wanted a better life, and I strongly believed that I could and would make that happen. My mother always told me that I was gifted, and I believed I was special. She consistently told me that I needed to get an education and that it would set me free. Despite not having any healthy role models to demonstrate a normal life for me, the love I had for my mom gave me hope that life would get better. Also, my demeanor has always been a sensitive and forgiving one—it's just who I am. I learned over time, through different experiences, that my parents did the best they could at the time with the tools they had to work with.

How hard was it to lose both of your parents before they turned 50?

It was very difficult to lose my mother. Just when I could make a real difference in her difficult, hard-lived life—and when I was financially able to make her life easier—she passed away. I do know that she was very proud of me, and that helped me cope with her loss. With my father, however, I felt more indifference than emotion after his death. I often felt that it was a mistake for him to have had such a large family he could not care or be present for. However, although it saddened me that he was so self-centered, I never believed he was a bad person.

It's easier to be angry and hate-filled than forgiving and understanding. How were you able to transition from a troubled childhood to a prosperous life?

I don't think I was ever angry or hate-filled. In spite of the time my sister and I spent in foster care—where we were both deeply hurt and scared—we knew our parents loved us and would never have treated us like the foster parents did. Knowing I was loved carried me through the down times in my life, including the knowledge that my lifestyle was not acceptable by many people's standards. I learned that loving and having confidence in myself would help me endure most challenges. I took on the attitude, and believed early on in the philosophy, that you can attract what you want and make it happen for yourself. Also, I adhere to the theory on abundance that I've been practicing for many, many years—the idea that there is enough of everything in this world for all of us, if we are willing to share. Gratitude is the basis for everything: be

ABOUT

the

AUTHOR

grateful for what you already have, see the miracles that come from that belief, dream big, construct an empowering reality, stop making excuses, realize your potential, attract opportunity, and commit to living your dream. My mantra is "BELIEVE, RECEIVE, BECOME."

Early in life you survived two major car accidents, one killing the driver of the car you were in. How did these brushes with death impact you?

I believe I gained a real respect for life. The accidents showed me at a young age how temporary life can be. Concerning the fatal accident that I was involved in during high school, I realized late that I had gone from talking and laughing in the car one moment, to surviving a tragic accident moments later. Having experienced several brushes with death, the precious nature of life became more and more apparent. I learned quickly to be grateful for life and to never take things for granted.

You reunited with both of your siblings who were adopted out. What is your relationship like with them today?

My sister and her family have been part of our lives for over twenty-five years, frequently coming to family gatherings and holidays, which has been wonderful. My brother, on the other hand, has chosen not to have an ongoing relationship, which has been deeply saddening.

You candidly discuss having sexual identity conflicts. How did that get resolved?

I believe it took time and feeling more confident with myself. Accomplishing and reaching my goals led to success, which in turn led to having a higher self-esteem.

Graduating from college empowered me to want and achieve more. I was the first person in my family at that time to finish a higher-education program. The climate at that time in society still had negative connotations attached to being gay, so I continued to live my life under the radar. As I grew older and experienced life and many cultures through travel, I grew to have more compassion and love for people and myself. I also embraced spiritual teachings and had a hunger to learn and absorb more.

Why do you say that one should never apologize for or hide who they are, just because people might be uncomfortable?

I didn't always believe in that philosophy. However, with social progression, changing norms, and a better understanding of my sexuality, I realized that I was far from alone. Having learned of the vastness of the gay community, and with a growing circle of friends both gay and straight, I learned that the people around me accepted me for who I truly am. This led to a full acceptance of myself. I always presented myself in a positive self-assured way.

Another message in your book is about thriving with cancer. Why didn't you accept your diagnosis as a death sentence?

Acceptance of the cancer in my body was never an option. I explored many different medical treatments, and after playing both sides of the medical world, I used and implemented the best treatments that served me and what I responded to. I decided on traditional medicine with a late-stage cancer diagnosis, but I believe good nutrition, exercise, supplements, and most of all a positive attitude, go a long way. Sunshine and love are some of the main ingredients in living a healthy, successful life, and a talented and open-minded physician is key.

A

B

O

U

T

t h e

A

U

T

H

O

R

The book also highlights your spiritual evolution, providing a deep reflection on your life's decisions. How hard is the process to take a deep introspective look at oneself?

When you are presented with a life-threatening disease, you start to reflect on your life and how you have lived it. It's not hard to process it because your options are limited. You can make the decision to learn, grow, and not accept the norm, using it to empower and conquer. Or, you can accept and believe what the experts tell you and live your life according to statistics: choosing not to grow or evolve and simply accept the outcome. I live life every day to the fullest. I wake up, put my right foot on the floor, and say "THANK," then my left foot hits the floor and I say "YOU." I also perform a daily ritual of affirmations. I welcome my journey and look forward to all the great things the universe presents.

*What follows is a paraphrased excerpt from a daily
practice I've embraced since my diagnosis, from the great
spiritual leader, Wayne Dyer.*

*I hope you find comfort and encouragement
in it as well.*

As you lie in bed, affirm: I am in perfect health, then notice how
that feels in your body. At first you will be calling upon your ego,
which believes that it is separate from God or the universal Source
of all, and an inner voice may say, *This is silly, I am sick, I am sore, I
am dying, or I am only fooling myself.* So simply dismiss these mind
viruses and conditioned memes . . .

You can quite readily break the habit of reviewing things that
are frustrating and upsetting before you sleep by using that time in
a positive way. Make this a sacred time to nurture thoughts that
align with powerful "I am" beliefs you have placed into your
imagination. When you see a tendency toward negativity, simply
pause and gently remind yourself in your sleepy state that you do
not wish to enter your unconscious world with these feelings. Then
assume the feeling in your body of your wish fulfilled, so that you
may enter your sleep with reminders to your subconscious to
automatically fulfill your life-enhancing wishes.

CPSIA information can be obtained
at www.ICGtesting.com
Printed in the USA
LVHW090829010519
615722LV00001B/12/P